The Golden Treasury of Patristic Quotations

Dr. I. D. E. Thomas

Other Books by Dr. Thomas

The Golden Treasury of Puritan Quotations

A Word from the Wise

The Hidden Hand

God's Outsider

On Trial

God's Harvest

Astrology and the Bible

The Omega Conspiracy

Puritan Daily Devotional Chronicles

 For information write: Hearthstone Publishing Ltd., 500 Beacon Drive, Oklahoma City, OK 73127.

ISBN 1-57558-005-5

Cover design by Eric Ferguson

For my wife Mildred

Table of Contents

Foreword

One day it dawned on me that I had largely missed the source material of early historical theology. As a doctoral student at Grace Theological Seminary in Winona Lake, Indiana, I had never extensively read the writings of those men who lived closest in time to the Apostles.

I can remember the joy of creating an opportunity to invade the patristic literature. A great gap in studies was bridged and my soul was enriched to read firsthand what these early saints had written. While I was appalled at times to see how quickly heresy came into the Church, yet I thrilled to encounter concise, simple, primitive affirmation of biblical truth.

To most of the twentieth century Christian community these treasures are lost. Only a few have enjoyed my doctoral experience. Thus, we are indebted to Dr. I. D. E. Thomas, who has labored on behalf of us all. Thousands of hours have been sacrificially invested in *The Golden Treasury of Patristic Quotations*. Thank you!

This delightful volume was not written primarily for scholars, but rather for those who otherwise would never drink at the well of writings served up by the early Church fathers. For busy pastors and speakers, this book serves as a seemingly exhaustless source of illustrations. The lay person will acquire a good survey of what the early Church believed. Seminarians and serious students will whet their appetite for the main courses from which the author obtained these taste treats.

Scores of theological topics have been carefully arranged in alphabetical order for easy access. You can read straight through from the beginning or randomly read those subjects of great interest to you. There is also an alphabetical index of authors quoted with brief biographical notes.

I salute you Dr. Thomas as a servant to modern Christendom for your diligent labors and valuable contribution to our reading what otherwise would have been too far off the beaten track for most Christian pilgrims to visit. I enthusiastically commend this anthology to space age saints who would have continued to miss a supremely important segment of Christian thought.

Dr. Richard Mayhue
Senior Vice-President & Dean
The Masters' Seminary
Sunland, California

Introduction

When I compiled *The Golden Treasury of Puritan Quotations,* I had been inspired to a prolonged study of the Puritans by men of the calibre of Dr. Martyn Lloyd-Jones and others. There were no such catalysts for this current study. As a matter of fact, it was our neglect of the early fathers that initially prompted my curiosity.

This study involved a venture into virgin territory as far as many evangelicals are concerned. The field had been left to Roman Catholic and Greek Orthodox believers. There is no question in my mind, however, that by such neglect evangelicals have deprived themselves of great and rare spiritual riches. They have closed their eyes to seven hundred years of unparalleled Church history.

The authors quoted in this book were heroic souls of the first degree. These patristic samurai blazed a trail for the Christian faith that was ultimately to capture cities, countries, even empires to the cause of Christ. The price they paid was a high one, in many instances the highest of all. Many of the men you meet here belonged to the "noble army of martyrs." You are rubbing shoulders with saints who suffered indescribable torments and tortures, and their deaths were among the cruelest ever perpetrated on humankind. In many cases, their persecutors were "aesthetes of torture"—with God's little flock on the receiving end. There is no question regarding their depth of conviction nor of their personal heroism.

Their freedom from the fear of death made them invincible. They challenged their very tormentors: "You can kill but not hurt us" (Justin Martyr). They stood their ground like the Theban Legion, not a single man yielding a single inch as they unflinchingly met their fate. They welcomed Sister Death as a shortcut to graduation. They understood Ignatius of Antioch when he issued his ultimatum: "I am the wheat of God, and let me be ground by the teeth of the wild beasts, that I may be found the pure bread of Christ."

Even a rationalist like W. E. H. Lecky had to admit that in those early centuries was seen "the most powerful moral lever that has ever been seen applied to the affairs of man."

To an evangelical, however, the preparation of this treasury has demanded much more selectivity than when compiling a treasury of the Puritans. The statements of the early fathers could not invariably be labelled as orthodox. In fact, some of their statements were plainly erroneous, and some border on the heretical. Caution had to be exercised even with men of the genius of Augustine, Origen, and Tertullian. Although timewise they lived close to the Apostolic age, their works do not reveal the same "infallible" quality.

Although all these men could be considered "saints" in the evangelical tradition, some of them would not qualify under the Roman Catholic definition of the term. Some have referred to crusty, old Jerome and his "abominable gift for invective." And others to the formidable Tertullian possessing "every virtue except moderation." William A. Jurgens rightly concludes: "No doubt the early Church venerated many as saints who could never have escaped the telling barbs of a devil's advocate."

In spite of such human frailties and foibles, they were all men who believed in Jesus and proudly bore His brand in a pagan and hostile society. Most of them were glad to sacrifice their lives for Him, believing martyrdom to be the supreme virtue.

Our part of the world has known very little, if any, persecution of the Christian faith. But how long will the summer last? There could be different days ahead with God winnowing His harvest and grading His little flock, by means of state and public persecution. If that should be the case, nothing could prepare one better than a thorough acquaintance with these mighty martyrs who withstood fire and flame, the rack and wild beasts without yielding one inch. By their witness they changed the world in the Name of the One who had first changed them. The dictum of T. R. Glover is still germane: "They out-fought, out-taught, out-lived, and out-died the pagan."

Although their writings fall short of the inspired books of the New Testament, nevertheless they possessed a merit of their own. We think in particular of those fathers who wrote during the golden age of patristic literature (313–461). These men could scale some high peaks, quite as high as some of the eminentoes of Periclean Greece or Augustan Rome. They succeeded in combining classical form with Christian content.

To him who has the time and the inclination to harvest these fertile fields of patristic thought, he will find himself moved and blessed beyond measure. Some of their work he will find timely, most of it timeless.

Abortion

You shall not procure an abortion or kill a newborn child.

—Didache

Murder?

Prevention of birth is premature murder.

—Tertullian, *The Christian Defence*

There are also women among you [pagans] who, by taking certain drugs destroy the beginnings of the future human being while it is still in the womb and are guilty of infanticide before they are mothers. . . .

—Minucius Felix, *Octavius*

A woman who has deliberately destroyed a fetus must pay the penalty for murder.

—Basil the Great, *Letter to Amphilochius, Bishop of Iconium*

It makes no difference whether it is a life already born that one snatches away or a life that is coming to birth that one destroys. The future man is a man already: the whole fruit is present in the seed.

—Tertullian, *The Christian Defence*

Some go so far as to take potion, that they may insure barrenness, and thus murder human beings almost before their conception. Some, when they find themselves with child through their sin, use drugs to procure abortion, and when (as often happens) they die with their offspring, they enter the lower world laden with the guilt not only of adultery against Christ but also of suicide and child murder.

—Jerome, *Letters to Eustochium*

When does life begin?

Life begins with conception, because we contend that the soul begins at conception. Life begins when the soul begins.

—Tertullian, *The Soul*

It seems very rash to deny that those fetuses ever lived, that are cut away and ejected limb by limb from wombs of the pregnant, lest the mothers perish too, if the fetuses be left there dead. But from whatever time a man begins to live, from that time on certainly he is able to die. . . .

—Augustine, *Enchiridion of Faith, Hope, and Love*

Those also who give drugs causing abortions are murderers themselves, as well as those who receive the poison which kills the fetus.

—Basil the Great, *Letters to Amphilochius, Bishop of Iconium*

Adoption

For all who believe in God are sons of God by adoption: but the only begotten alone is Son by nature.

—John Cassian, *The Seven Books*

Adversity

Look for hidden lessons

When He exposes us to adversities, it is either to prove our perfections or correct our imperfections.

—Augustine, *The City of God*

The suffering of adversity does not degrade you but exalts you; human tribulation teaches you, it does not destroy you.

—Isidore of Seville, *A Dialogue between the Erring Soul and Reason*

Troubles such as we are going through give opportunity to prove and to improve ourselves.

—Ignatius, *Letter to the Ephesians*

Secret recipe of the saints

Do not let anything catch your eye besides Him, for whom I carry around these chains—my spiritual pearls!

—Ignatius, *Letter to the Ephesians*

Above all, we ought to endure everything for God's sake so that He may also endure us.

—Ignatius, *Letters to Polycarp*

And thus it is that in the same affliction the wicked detest God and blaspheme, while the good pray and praise. So material a difference does it make, not what ills are suffered, but what kind of man suffers them. For, stirred up with the same movement, mud exhales a horrible stench, and ointment emits a fragrant odour.

—Augustine, *City of God*

If, when you are ill-treated, you show gentleness, the whole glory of your victory is attributed to Him; but, if you stand up against your enemy and fight him, the victory is yours to be sure, but the Shepherd is hidden.

—John Chrysostom, *Homilies on Matthew*

The saints, however, do not wither in the face of trials.

—Athanasius, *Resurrection Letter XII*

Angels

Distinctives

. . . secondary Splendours . . . the Ministers of the Primary Splendour.

—Gregory of Nazianzus, *On the Theophany.*

An angel . . . is an intelligent being, ever in motion, with free will, incorporeal, ministering to God, having by grace obtained immortality in his nature, the form and limitation of whose essence is known to the Creator alone.

—John Damascene, *The Source of Knowledge*

The angels are spirits; but it is not because they are spirits that they are angels. It is when they are sent, that they become angels. For angel is the name of an office, not of a nature. . . . By reason of what they are, they are spirits. By reason of what they do, they are angels.

—Augustine, *Psalms*

. . . secondary intelligent lights, having their light from the First Light, who is without beginning. They have no need of speech and hearing, for without uttered word they impart to each other their own thoughts and purposes.

—John Damascene, *The Source of Knowledge*

The perfection of angels, moreover, is sanctification and perseverance therein.

—Basil the Great, *The Holy Spirit*

This is how they differ from the Holy Spirit; His nature is holiness, whereas the holiness that is in the angels is there by reason of their participating in it.

—Basil the Great, *The Holy Spirit*

⇹ Their service

They are sent for the sake of those who will inherit salvation.

—Hilary of Poitiers, *Commentaries on the Psalms*

It is not the nature of God, but the weakness of men, which requires their service.

—Hilary of Poitiers, *Commentaries on the Psalms*

They sing the praises of the divine majesty and contemplate eternally the eternal glory, not that God may thereby have an increase of glory, for nothing can be added to what is already full . . . but that there may never be an end of blessing to those first natures after God.

—Gregory of Nazianzus, *Second Theological Oration*

⇹ Their creation

The Word, before ever men were made, was the Creator of the angels.

—Tatian the Syrian, *Address to the Greeks*

In the creation of the angels, I would have you recall that their original cause is the Father, their creating cause is the Son, and their perfecting cause the Spirit.

—Basil the Great, *The Holy Spirit*

Superior to man?

. . . incomparably far above us in respect to their knowledge. Certainly they are more extended interiorly and exteriorly in knowing, because they contemplate the Font itself of Knowledge.

—Gregory the Great, *Moral Teachings from Job*

Fallen angels

Angels, who renounced the beauty of God for a beauty which fades, and so fell from heaven to earth.

—Clement of Alexandria, *The Instructor*

The Creator of all goods granted no grace for the reparation of the wicked angels, should it not rather be our understanding that their guilt was judged to be all the more damnable as their nature was the more sublime?

—Augustine, *Homilies on John*

The more superior is a rational nature, so much the worse is its ruin; and the more unbelievable is its sin, so much the more damnable it is.

—Augustine, *Against Julian's Second Reply*

He was bound to turn the apostate angel away even because when this latter fell it was in spite of a constant strength in which it bore nothing of the weakness of flesh.

—Gregory the Great, *Moral Teachings from Job*

"They shall be as angels": thus while likeness to the angels is promised identity with them is refused.

—Jerome, *Letter to Theodora*

An unusual exposition

It pleased God, the Creator and Governor of the universe, that since the whole body of the angels had not fallen into rebellion, the part of them which had fallen should remain in perdition eternally, and that the other part . . . should rejoice in the sure and certain knowledge of their eternal happiness; but that, on the other hand, mankind, who constituted the remainder of the intelligent creation, having perished without exception under sin, both original and actual, and the consequent punishments, should be in part restored, and should fill up the gap which the rebellion and fall of the devils had left in the company of the angels. For this is the promise to the saints, that at the resurrection they shall be equal to the angels of God. . . . We do not know the number either of the saints or of the devils; but we know that the children of the holy mother who was called barren on earth shall succeed to the place of the fallen angels, and shall dwell for ever in that peaceful abode from which they fell.

—Augustine, *Enchiridion*

Anger

We have, it must be admitted, a use for anger excellently implanted in us for which alone it is useful and profitable for us to admit it, viz., when we are indignant and rage against the lustful emotions of our heart. . . .

—John Cassian, *The Institutes*

When anyone is overcome by a wrong, and blazes up in a fire of anger, we should not hold that the bitterness of the insult offered to him is the *cause* of his sin, but rather the *manifestation* of a secret weakness. . . .

—John Cassian, *Conference of Abbot Piamun*

God's hottest anger against sinners is when He shows no anger.

—Jerome, *Letter to Castrutius*

Antichrist

(In the Scriptures) the name is suppressed, because it is not worthy of being proclaimed by the Holy Spirit.

—Irenaeus, *Against Heresies*

Imitation but diametrically different

Now, as our Lord Jesus Christ . . . who was prophesied of under the figure of a lion, on account of His royalty and glory, in the same way have the Scriptures also aforetime spoken of Antichrist as a lion, on account of his tyranny and violence.

—Hippolytus, *Treatise on Christ and Antichrist*

Limits

But thanks be to God who has confined the greatness of that tribulation to a few days; for He says, "But for the elect's sake those days shall be shortened"; and the Antichrist shall reign only three and a half years—a times, and a dividing of times.

—Cyril of Jerusalem, *Catechetical Lectures*

Jeremiah speaks of him thus in a parable: "The partridge cried, gathered what he did not hatch, making himself riches without judgment. . . ."

The partridge is a vainglorious creature, when it sees near at hand the nest of another partridge with young in it, and with the parent-bird away on the wing in quest of food, it imitates the cry of the other bird, and calls the young to itself; and they, taking it to be their own parent, run to it. And it delights itself proudly in the alien pullets as in its own. But when the real parent-bird returns, and calls them with its own familiar cry, the young recognize it, and forsake the deceiver. . . . This thing, then, the prophet has adopted as a simile, applying it in a similar manner to Antichrist. For he will allure mankind to himself, wishing to gain possession of those who are not his own, and promising deliverance to all, while he is unable to save himself.

—Hippolytus, *Treatise of Christ and Antichrist*

Superlative martyrs

I consider that the martyrs of that season will be greater than all martyrs; for the former martyrs wrestled with man only; but these, in the time of the Antichrist, will battle with Satan himself in person.

—Cyril of Jerusalem, *Catechetical Lectures*

Warning

I fear the wars of the nations; I fear the divisions among Christians; I fear the hatred among brethren. Enough! But God forbid that it should be fulfilled in our days. However, let us be prepared.

—Cyril of Jerusalem, *Catechetical Lectures*

For if thou believest not in Christ, much more oughtest thou not to believe in Antichrist.

—John Chrysostom, *Homilies on Thessalonians*

Daniel has spoken, therefore, of two abominations; the one of destruction, and the other of desolation. What is that of destruction, but that which Antiochus established there at the time? And what is that of desolation, but that which shall be universal when Antichrist comes?

—Hippolytus, *Commentary on the Visions of Daniel*

Bottom line

Truly Jesus Christ will extinguish by His presence the last persecution which is to be made by the Antichrist.

—Augustine, *The City of God*

Antichrist is coming, but above him comes Christ also.

—Cyprian, *Epistles*

How would we ever expect to be long-suffering if we had not faced the opposition of antichrists?

—Athanasius, *Resurrection Letter VIII*

Atheism

So, then, we are called atheists. We confess that we are atheists as far as false gods are concerned but not with respect to the true God.

—Justin, *First Apology*

Atonement

(The devil) dragged the human race into a perpetual captivity by the heavy debt of inherited liability which the author of the debt transmitted to his posterity as their inherited debt. The Lord Jesus came and offered His death in place of the death of all, and poured out His blood in place of the blood of everyone.

—Ambrose of Milan, *Letter to his sister Marcellina*

Never, therefore, is sin spared, because never is it forgiven without having been avenged.

—Gregory the Great, *Moral Teachings from Job*

The Sacrificial Victim was offered for all mankind, and was sufficient to save all; but it is believers alone who enjoy the bounty thereof.

—John Chrysostom, *Homilies on the Epistle to the Galatians*

After His public ministry, He did not eat of the lamb, but Himself suffered as the true Lamb in the Paschal feast. . . .

—Peter of Alexandria, *Fragments*

N.B.

. . . the Lamb, that had come to set free the flocks and the oxen from sacrifices.

—Ephraim the Syrian, *Hymns on the Nativity*

Baptism

. . . the virtue of Baptism is to be understood as a covenant with God for a second life. . . .

—Gregory of Nazianzus, *Oration on Holy Baptism*

This and much more

For prisoners, Baptism is ransom, forgiveness of debts, death of sin, regeneration of the soul, a resplendent garment, an unbreakable seal, a chariot to heaven, a protector royal, a gift of adoption.

—Basil the Great, *Sermon on Baptism*

Who therefore, says that sins are not entirely forgiven in Baptism, let him say that the Egyptians did not really die in the Red Sea.

—Gregory the Great, *Letter to Theoctista*

In whose Name?

In whose name were you baptized? In the Father's name? Jewish, but good. In the Son's name? Good; no longer Jewish, but not yet perfect. In the Holy Spirit's name? Excellent! This is perfect!

—Gregory of Nazianzus, *Against the Arians and About Myself*

Let no one be misled by the fact that the Apostle frequently omits the name of the Father and of the Holy Spirit when mentioning baptism; nor let anyone suppose that the invocation of the Names is a matter of indifference. "Those of you," he says, "who have been baptized in Christ have put on Christ," and again, "Those of you who have been baptized in Christ have been baptized in His death." The naming of Christ, you see, is the confession of the whole; it bespeaks the God who anoints, the Son who is anointed, and the Spirit who is the anointing.

—Basil the Great, *The Holy Spirit*

It is quite proper that but one name is spoken of when it is said: "In the *name* of the Father and of the Son and of the Holy Spirit," so that faith is posited in one principal authority of the perfect and indivisible Trinity.

—Faustinus, *The Trinity*

(Baptism) is complete if you confess Father, Son, and Holy Spirit. If you deny one, you undermine the whole.

—Ambrose of Milan, *The Holy Spirit*

The Backslider

(He) who has been baptized in the Church, should he become a deserter from the Church, will lack holiness but will not lack the seal of the sacrament. . . . Just as the man who is a deserter from the army loses legal status without losing his citizenship.

—Augustine, *Sermon to the Newly Baptized on the Octave of Easter*

Water and Spirit

If your piety is unfeigned the Holy Spirit will come down upon you also, and from on high a paternal voice will sound over you: not, "This is My Son," but "This is now become My son." The "is" belongs to Him alone . . . because always the Son of

God He is. To you belongs the "is now become," because you have sonship not by nature, but have received it by adoption.

—Cyril of Jerusalem, *Catechetical Lectures*

This then is what it means to be born again of water and Spirit; just as our dying is effected in the water, our living is wrought through the Spirit. If, therefore, there is any grace in the water, it is not from the nature of water but from the Spirits's presence there.

—Basil the Great, *The Holy Spirit*

Since man is of twofold nature, composed of body and soul, the purification also is twofold: . . . The water cleanses the body, and the Spirit seals the soul.

—Cyril of Jerusalem, *Catechetical Lectures*

Re-baptism?

If the one and true Baptism did not exist except in the Church, surely it would not exist in those who depart from her unity. But it does exist in these; for upon returning they do not receive it again, for the very reason that on leaving they did not lose it. . . .

—Augustine, *Baptism*

Would it be necessary to be circumcised again? . . .

—Augustine, *Against the Letter of Petilian*

Those whom Judas baptized were not baptized again.

—Augustine, *Homilies on John*

Triple immersion

In respect to the triple immersion of Baptism, no truer response can be given than . . . that where there is one faith a variation in usage does no harm to Holy Church.

—Gregory the Great, *Letter to Leander, Bishop of Seville*

Baptism of blood

(Beside the Baptisms of Moses, John and Jesus,) I know also a fourth Baptism, that by martyrdom and blood, by which also Christ Himself was baptized. This one is far more august than the others, since it cannot be defiled by later stains.

—Gregory of Nazianzus, *Oration on the Holy Lights*

Unworthy celebrant?

All the Sacraments, while they are injurious to those who administer them unworthily, are beneficial to those who receive them worthily.

—Augustine, *Against the Letter of Parmenian.*

In so far as I can judge, it is already as clear as crystal that in this question of Baptism what is to be considered is not who confers but what is conferred; not who receives but what is received; not who has it but what he has.

—Augustine, *Baptism*

It is God who controls what is His own.

—Optatus of Milevis, *Against Parmenian*

The Bible

Divinely Inspired

They were spoken and written by God, through men who spoke of God.

—Athanasius, *Incarnation of the Word*

The sacred Scriptures come from the fullness of the Spirit; so that there is nothing in the Prophets, or the Law, or the Gospel, or the Epistles, which descends not from divine majesty.

—Origen

If their age does not prove the Scriptures divine, then their majesty does.

—Tertullian, *Apology*

In an ecstasy beyond their natural powers of reasoning, and moved by the Divine Spirit, (the prophets) spoke out the things with which they had been possessed, the Spirit making use of them after the manner of a flute-player breathing into a flute.

—Athenagoras of Athens, *Supplication for the Christians*

I suggest that the fulfillment of prophecy is sufficient witness to the divine origin thereof.

—Tertullian, *Apology*

The wisdom of God pervades every divinely inspired writing, reaching out to each single letter.

—Origen, *Commentaries on the Psalms*

He is the Author of both Testaments, because the New is prefigured in the Old, and the Old is unveiled in the New.

—Augustine, *Against an Adversary of the Law and the Prophets*

Inerrant

We must surrender ourselves to the authority of Holy Scripture, for it can neither mislead nor be misled.

—Augustine

There is nothing wrong or misleading written in it.

—Clement, *Letter to the Church in Corinth*

For if we once admit in that supreme monument of authority even one polite lie, no shred of those books will remain.

—Augustine, *Letter to Jerome*

The teaching, which is according to the Saviour, is complete in itself and without defect.

—Clement of Alexandria, *The Stromata*

Neither does Scripture falsify anything, nor does the Holy Spirit deceive His servants. . . .

—Hippolytus, *Commentary on Daniel*

We who extend the accuracy of the Spirit to every letter and serif (of Scripture) will never admit, for it were impious to do so, that even the smallest matters were recorded in a careless and hasty manner by those who wrote them down.

—Gregory of Nazianzus, *In Defence of His Flight to Pontus*

To the canonical Scriptures alone I owe agreement without dissent.

—Augustine

Nothing of discrepancy will be found in Sacred Scripture.

—Epiphanius, *Panacea Against All Heresies*

For His word cannot deceive; but our senses are easily cheated. His word has never failed; our senses err most of the time.

—John Chrysostom, *Homilies on the Gospel of Matthew*

"But they were written by unlearned and ignorant men, and should not therefore be readily believed." See that this be not rather a stronger reason for believing that they have not been adultered by any false statements, but were put forth by men of simple mind, who knew not how to trick out their tales with meretricious ornaments.

—Arnobius, *Against the Heathen*

I do most firmly believe that none of their authors has erred in anything that he has written therein.

—Augustine, *Letter to Jerome*

Its finality

After Jesus Christ, there is no need of further search; nor after the Gospel, is there any further inquiry. In as much as we believe, we desire nothing further to believe. For beyond what we already have, we believe there is nothing further that we ought to believe.

—Tertullian, *The Demurrer Against the Heretics*

I do not accept what you introduce apart from Scripture. . . .

—Tertullian, *The Flesh of Christ*

Biblical contradictions?

Since I am totally convinced that no Scripture is contradictory to another, I shall admit instead that I do not understand what is spoken of, and shall strive to persuade those who assume that the Scriptures are contradictory to be rather of the same opinion as myself.

—Justin Martyr, *Dialogue with Trypho the Jew*

If I find anything in those writings which seem to be contrary to the truth, I presume that either the codex is inaccurate, or the translator has not followed what was said, or I have not properly understood it. . . .

—Augustine, *Letter to Jerome*

Whatever we read in the Old Testament we find also in the Gospel; and what we read in the Gospel is deduced from the Old Testament. There is no discord between them, no disagreement.

—Jerome, *Letter to Pope Damasus*

We are able by the grace of God to explain some of them, while we must leave others in the hands of God, and that not only in the present world, but also in that which is to come, so that God should for ever teach, and that man should for ever learn the things taught him by God.

—Irenaeus, *Against Heresies*

"The Evangelists, . . ." it may be said, "are in many places found to disagree with each other." Yet, this very thing is a great proof of their truthfulness. For if they had agreed exactly in all respects, even as to time and place to the using of the same words, none of our enemies would believe that they had not met together and had not written what they wrote in accord with some human compact; for such perfect agreement could not have come from candidness. But as it is, the discord which seems to be present in little matters shields them from every suspicion and clearly vindicates the character of the writers.

—John Chrysostom, *Homilies on the Gospel of Matthew*

Manipulating the Scriptures

He who wrests the words of the Lord according to his own pleasure, and saith there is no resurrection and judgment, is the first-born of Satan.

—Polycarp, *Letter to the Smyrnaens*

It cannot be denied that this tearing asunder of the faith has arisen from the defect of poor intelligence, which twists what is read to conform to its opinion, instead of adjusting its opinion to the meaning of what is read.

—Hilary of Poitiers, *The Trinity*

Yes, and the robber is skilled in Scripture.

—Gregory of Nazianzus, *Oration on Holy Baptism*

You shall not abandon the commandments of the Lord; but

you shall keep what you have received, adding nothing to it nor taking anything.

—Didache

Do not be lead astray by winning words and clever arguments. Even to me, who tell you these things, do not give ready belief, unless you receive from the Holy Scriptures the proof of the things which I announce.

—Cyril of Jerusalem, *Catechetical Lectures*

Ignorance of the Scripture is ignorance of Christ.

—Jerome

Biblical Obscurities?

Our faith is fed by what is plain in Scripture and tried by what is obscure.

—Augustine

Biblical exegesis?

Explain the Scriptures by the Scriptures.

—Clement of Alexandria

Do you suppose that we would ever have been able to grasp the truths set forth in the Scriptures if the grace of understanding had not been given to us by the will of Him who wanted to reveal them?

—Justin, *Dialogue with Trypho the Jew*

If you believe what you like in the gospel, and reject what you dislike, it is not the gospel you believe, but yourself.

—Augustine, *Against Faustus the Manichean*

There are two things on which all interpretation of Scripture depends: the mode of ascertaining the proper meaning, and the mode of making known the meaning when it is ascertained.

—Augustine, *On Christian Doctrine*

Going deeper

Seek and find, and realize that the truth does not lie openly on the surface.

—Clement, *Homily III*

The hearer of God's Word ought to be like those animals that chew the cud; he ought not only feed upon it, but to ruminate upon it.

—Augustine

Study your heart in the light of the Holy Scripture, and you will know therein who you were, who you are, and who you ought to be.

—Fulgence of Ruspe, *Letter to Senator Theodore*

We draw codices from enemies in order to refute other enemies. . . . A Jew carries the codex, by which the Christian may believe. They have become our librarians, just as servants are accustomed to carry codices behind their masters; and the former faint by carrying them while the latter grow strong by reading them.

—Augustine, *Psalms*

N.B.

Had we not known the Word and been illuminated by Him, we would have been no different from fowls that are being fed, fattened in darkness and nourished for death.

—Clement of Alexandria, *Exhortation to the Greeks*

Blood of Christ

(See also: Atonement, Cross, Death of Christ)

To whom was the Blood paid out that was shed for us, and why was it shed? . . . We were in bondage to the Evil One, sold under sin, and receiving pleasure in exchange for wickedness. If a ransom belongs not to someone else but to him who holds in bondage, I ask you, to whom was this paid, and for what reason? If to the Evil One, O, what an outrage! . . . If to the Father, first I ask, how can that be? For we were not being detained by Him; and second, why would He be delighted by the Blood of His Only-begotten Son? . . . Surely it is evident, however, that the Father did receive (the sacrifice of His Son), though neither asking nor demanding it, but because of His plan of redemption and so that might we be sanctified by the Humanity of God.

—Gregory of Nazianzus, *Second Oration on Easter*

Carnality

I (did) not press on to enjoy my God, but was borne up to Thee by Thy beauty, and soon borne down from Thee by mine own weight, sinking with sorrow into these inferior things. This weight was carnal custom.

—Augustine, *Confessions*

Chastisement

It is better to be punished and cleansed now than to be sent to the torment to come, when it will be time for punishing only, and not for cleansing.

—Gregory of Nazianzus, *On the Destruction of the Crops by Hail*

Oft doth the father of a family command his sons to be corrected by the most worthless slaves; though he designeth the heritage for the former, fetters for the latter.

—Augustine, *On the Psalms*

Chastity

(See also: Virginity)

Chastity, the sacred stole of the body.

—Clement of Alexandria, *The Instructor*

We are all of us the temple of God as soon as the Holy Spirit has entered into us; but the sacristan priestess of the temple is Chastity, who must allow nothing unclean or profane to enter.

—Tertullian, *On Female Dress*

In fact, so far from us is the desire for incest, that some blush even at the thought of a chaste union.

—Minucius Felix, *Octavius*

They (Christians) have a common table, but no common bed.

—Tertullian, *Apology*

For Christian chastity it is not enough to be; it wishes also to be seen.

—Tertullian, *On Female Dress*

For so great is the influence of probity and chastity that all men, or almost all men, are moved by praise of these virtues; nor is any man so depraved by vice, but he hath some feeling of honour left in him.

—Augustine, *City of God*

While you maintain perfect chastity, do not be puffed up in vain conceit against those who walk a humbler path in matrimony. . . . Were you not born of those who had married? . . . Because you have a possession of gold do not on that account hold the silver in contempt.

—Cyril of Jerusalem, *Catechetical Lectures*

N.B.

As a widow, the second degree of chastity is hers.

—Jerome, *Letter to Eustochium*

Give me chastity and continency—but not yet!

—Augustine, *Confessions*

Christ

Who is He?

This is He who in Abel was slain, in Isaac was bound, who in Jacob dwelt in a strange land, who in Joseph was sold, who in Moses was cast out, in the lamb was sacrificed, and in David was hunted, in the prophets was dishonoured.

—Melito of Sardis, *Paschal Homily*

The Galilean who had ascended to the third heaven.

—Lucian

He is called by many names. But we shall leave aside all of them and prove that He who came from God is God and the Son of God.

—Aphraates, *Treatises*

He sent (to us) the very Designer and Creator of the universe Himself, through whom He had made the heavens, and by whom He had enclosed the sea within its own bounds; whose mysteries all the elements of nature faithfully guard; from whom the sun received the schedule of its daily flight; whose command the moon obeys in lighting up the night; to whom the stars give heed in following the path of the moon; by whom all things were ordered and bounded and placed in subjection.

—Letter to Diognetus

He is All in all: Patriarch among the patriarchs; Law in the laws; Chief Priest among priests; Ruler among kings; the Prophet among prophets; the Angel among angels; the Man among men; Son in the Father; God in God: King to all eternity.

—Irenaeus, *Fragments from Lost Writings*

Between Father and Son is the plain distinction that comes of generation; (Begetter and begotten *must* be personally distinct); so that Christ is God of God, Everlasting, Fulness of Fulness.

—Ambrose of Milan, *Rules for Christian Living*

So far as He is God, He and the Father are one; so far as He is man, the Father is greater than He.

—Augustine, *Enchiridion*

One Son of God, and at the same time Son of Man; one Son of Man, and at the same time Son of God; not two Sons of God, God and Man, but one Son of God: God without beginning; Man with a beginning, our Lord Jesus Christ.

—Augustine, *Enchiridion*

The Christ was twofold: Man is what was seen, but God is what was not seen. As Man, He truly ate as we do . . . as God, He fed the five thousand with five loaves.

—Cyril of Jerusalem, *Catechetical Lectures*

The Son of God born of the Virgin did not first become the Son of God when He became Son of Man; but already being the Son of God, He then became the Son of Man.

—Hilary of Poitiers, *Commentaries on the Psalms*

All victorious

Thou hast conquered, O Galilean.

—Julian the apostate, his dying words

He descended, indeed, into Hades alone, but He arose accompanied by a multitude; and rent asunder that means of separation which had existed from the beginning of the world, and cast down its partition-wall.

—Ignatius, *Letter to the Trallians*

The priests indeed, and the ministers of the Word, are good; but the High Priest is better. . . .

—Ingatius, *Letter to the Philadelphians*

Omnipresent

Being always everywhere, and being contained nowhere.

—Clement of Alexandria, *The Stromata*

Christ . . . was at one and the same time with the apostles and with the angels; in the Father and in the uttermost parts of the sea. So afterwards He was with Thomas in India, with Peter at Rome, with Paul in Illyricum, with Titus in Crete, with Andrew in Achaia.

—Jerome, *Letter to Marcella*

Omniscient

It is plain that as the Word He knows also the hour and the end of all things, although as man He is ignorant of it.

—Athanasius, *Discourses Against the Arians*

Sinless

How could Christ have died for sinners if He Himself were in sin?

—John Chrysostom, *Homilies on the First Epistle to the Corinthians*

Finality

A law set down after another law abrogates that which was before it, and a covenant made later likewise voids that which was earlier, an eternal and final law, the Christ, is given to us, a faithful covenant after which there shall be no law, no precept, no commandment.

—Justin, *Dialogue with Trypho the Jew*

After Christ not a single prophet appeared among you Jews.

—Justin, *Dialogue with Trypho the Jew*

Son of God and Son of Man

Thus too is the Lord of glory said to have been crucified, even though His divine nature endured no suffering; and thus too is the Son of Man confessed to be in heaven before the suffering.

—John Damascene, *The Source of Knowledge*

He is called Son because He is identical to the Father in essence; and not only this, but also because He is of Him. He is called Only-begotten not because He is singular Son, Son of a singular, and Son singular, but because He is Son in a singular fashion and not in a corporeal way.

—Gregory of Nazianzus, *Fourth Theological Oration*

In all except sin He was made man.

—Gregory of Nazianzus, *On the Theophany of Christ*

I am saying God *and* Man. But whenever you attribute the sufferings to the flesh and the miracles to God, you must necessarily, whether you want to or not, attribute the humble words to the Man born of Mary, but the more sublime and divinely suitable, to the Word who existed in the beginning.

—Amphilochius of Iconium, *Fragments*

"In the beginning was the Word:" behold Him to whom Mary hearkened; "and the Word was made flesh: " behold Him whom Martha served.

—Augustine

This is the Holy Savior who came down from heaven, who deigned to fashion our salvation in a virginal workshop . . .

who did not change His nature when He took on humanity along with His divinity.

—Epiphanius, *The Man Well-Anchored*

He Himself who was before the ages from the Father without a mother is He Himself who at the end of the ages is from the Mother without a father.

—Gregory the Great, *Moral Teaching from Job*

His divine generation

(Divine generation) is a thing the full nature of which the human mind is incapable of understanding by any investigative process; by faith, however, it is grasped in its fullness. For even if I am not permitted to know how He was born, neither am I permitted to be ignorant of the fact that He was born.

—Ambrose of Milan, *Commentary on the Gospel of Luke*

The course of His generation I do not know, but the Author of His generation I do know.

—Ambrose of Milan, *Commentary on the Gospel of Luke*

Great is the mystery . . .

The Son of God is dead: and it is believable, because it is folly. And having been buried, He rose again: it is certain, because it is impossible.

—Tertullian, *The Flesh of Christ*

O mystic wonder! The Lord was laid low, and man rose up!

—Clement of Alexandria, *Exhortation to the Greeks*

Why is Christ man and Son of Man, if in Him there is nothing of man and nothing from man?

—Tertullian, *The Flesh of Christ*

Does it seem to you to be vain and of no consequence, and do you think it a small thing and no divine miracle that all mankind hastens to the name of one Crucified Man?

—Augustine, *Faith in Things Unseen*

The same one is Priest and Sacrifice, the same one is God and Temple: the Priest, *through whom* we are reconciled; the Sacrifice, *by which* we are reconciled; the Temple, *in which* we are reconciled; and the God, *to whom* we are reconciled.

—Fulgence of Ruspe, *The Rule of Faith*

He who has really grasped what Jesus said can appreciate His silence.

—Ignatius, *Letter to the Ephesians*

For I know not how to make a separation between Christ and God, I cannot insert blasphemous distinctions between Jesus and God, or rend my Lord asunder from Himself.

—John Cassian, *The Seven Books*

He who is hungry, and yet maintains myriads; who is weary, and yet gives rest to the weary; who has not where to lay His head, and yet bears up all things in His hand; who suffers, and yet heals sufferings; who is smitten, and yet confers liberty on the world; who is pierced in the side, and yet repairs the side of Adam.

—Hippolytus, *Discourse on the Holy Theophany*

He, through whom time was made, was made in time; and He, older by eternity than the world itself, was younger in age than many of His servants in the world; He, who made man, was made man; He was given existence by a mother whom He brought into existence; He was carried in hands which He formed; He nursed at breasts which He filled; He cried like a babe in the manger in speechless infancy—this Word without which human eloquence is speechless!

—Augustine, *Sermon on Christmas*

N.B.

For it is devoid of sense, and a mark of great ignorance, to affirm that He who is the cause of everything is posterior to the origin of that thing.

—Alexander of Alexandria, *Epistles on the Arian Heresy*

The Lord withdraws when He is denied.

—Cyprian, *On the Unity of the Church*

This Christ, when He was come, the Jews denied, but the devils confessed . . . the Chief-priest knew Him not, and the devils confessed Him.

—Cyril of Jerusalem, *Lecture X*

Christians

Lambs of the royal flock.

—Clement of Alexandria, *The Instructor*

The name

My first and chosen name is Christian. But if you are asking for my name in the world, then I call myself Carpus.

—The martyr Carpus, examined by the Roman proconsul in Pergamum

It becomes evident that the entire crime with which they charge us does not consist in any wicked acts, but in the bearing of a name. The issue is not the name of a crime, but the crime of bearing a name.

—Tertullian, *To the Heathen*

We should not be hated and punished because we are called Christians, for what has a name to do with our being criminals?

—Athenagoras, *A Plea Regarding Christians*

It is fitting, then, not only to be called Christians, but to be so in reality. For it is not the being called so, but the being really so, that renders a man blessed.

—Ignatius, *Epistle to the Magnesians*

And what shall we say of the new race of us Christians, whom Christ at His advent planted in every country and in every region? For, lo, wherever we are, we are called after the one name of Christ—namely, Christians.

—Bardesanes, *Concering Fate*

I cannot call myself anything else than what I am, a Christian.

—Perpetua, testifying to her father before her martydom

Distinctives

Christians are not born but made.

—Jerome, *Letter to Laeta*

Men are not born Christians but become such.

—Tertullian, *Apology*

They have a common table, but no common bed. They are in the flesh, but they do not live according to the flesh. They live on earth, but their citizenship is in Heaven. They obey the established laws, but through their way of life they surpass these laws. They love all men and are persecuted by all. Nobody knows them, and yet they are condemned. They are put to death, and just through this they are brought to life. They are as poor as beggars, and yet they make many rich.

—*Letter to Diognetus*

Every foreign place is their fatherland, and every fatherland is to them a foreign place.

—*Letter to Diognetus*

I really believe that God does reside in some human beings.

—Sulpitius Severus, *Letter to Claudia*

Our mode of life is not to accustom us to voluptuousness and licentiousness, nor to the opposite extreme, but to the medium between these, that which is harmonious and temperate, and free of either evil, luxury, and parsimony.

—Clement of Alexandria, *The Instructor*

They converse as those who are aware that God is listening.

—Tertullian, *Apology*

To put it briefly, what the soul is in the body, that the Christians are in the world. . . . The soul dwells in the body, but it is not of the body; and Christians dwell in the world, though they are not of the world.

—*Letter to Diognetus*

Their first lawgiver taught them that they were all brothers.

—Lucian, *The Death of Peregrinus*

Power of the saints

The mystics say that it was by his word alone that Moses slew the Egyptian; as certainly afterwards it is related in the Acts that (Peter) slew with his word those who kept back part of the price of the land, and lied.

—Clement of Alexandria, *Fragments*

Let nothing glitter in your eyes apart from Him. . . .

—Ignatius, *Letter to the Ephesians*

Firstly, they derive their existence from God the Father; secondly, their rational nature from the Word; thirdly, their holiness from the Holy Spirit. . . .

—Origen, *De Principiis*

One with Christ

Notice carefully that in the case of Adam and Eve it is not said that these twain shall be a single spirit, nor a single soul, but that these twain shall be one flesh. Elsewhere, the just man, while remaining distinct from Christ, is said by the Apostle to be "one" in his relation with Christ: "for he that is joined unto the Lord is one spirit with Him."

—Origen, *On the Soul*

N.B.

Be pleasing to Him whose soldiers you are, and whose pay you receive. May none of you be found to be a deserter. Let your baptism be your armament; your faith, your helmet; your love, your spear; your endurance, your full suit of armour.

—Ignatius, *Letter to Polycarp*

Church

The true Israel

We who have been led to God through this crucified Christ, we are the true Israel of the Spirit, the real descendants of Judah, Jacob, Isaac and Abraham, who though uncircumcised was approved and blessed by God because of his faith and was called to be the father of many nations.

—Justin, *Dialogue with Trypho the Jew*

For if we hold with a firm heart the grace of God which hath been given us, we are Israel, the seed of Abraham. . . .

—Augustine, *Psalms*

Importance of the Church

He can no longer have God for his Father, who has not the Church for his mother.

—Cyprian

Let us love our Lord God, let us love His Church; Him as a Father, her as a Mother.

—Augustine, *Psalms*

Make no mistake about it. If anyone is not inside the sanctuary, he lacks God's bread.

—Ignatius, *Letter to the Ephesians*

If anyone outside the ark of Noah was able to escape, then perhaps someone outside the pale of the Church may escape.

—Cyprian

Unity of the Church

The unity of the Church is proved by the mutuality of the greetings of peace, by the use of the name "brother," and by mutual hospitality.

—Tertullian, *The Prescription of Heretics*

Church divisions

Nothing will so avail to divide the Church as love of power.

—John Chrysostom

He cannot possess the robe of Christ who rends and divides the Church of Christ.

—Cyprian, *On the Unity of the Catholic Church*

Her dowery?

The spouse of Christ, on whose account He poured out His own blood, as her marriage portion, that He might redeem her.

—Ignatius, *Epistle to the Philadelphians*

Fellowship

If any man follows him that separates from the truth, he shall not inherit the Kingdom of God, and if any man does not stand aloof from the preacher of falsehood, he shall be condemned to hell. For it is obligatory neither to separate from the godly, nor to associate with the ungodly.

—Ignatius, *Epistle to the Philadelphians*

Mixed fellowship

As long as she is a stranger in the world, the city of God has in her communion, and bound to her by the sacraments, some who shall not eternally dwell in the lot of the saints. Of these, some are not now recognized; others declare themselves, and do not hesitate to make common cause with our enemies in murmuring against God, whose sacramental badge they wear. These men you may today see thronging the churches with us, tomorrow crowding the theatres with the godless.

—Augustine, *The City of God*

The Church herself, which should be the appeaser of God in all things, what is she but the exasperator of God?

—Salvian, *The Governance of God*

If we bear in mind that Satan was chosen among the angels, and Judas among the apostles, and Nicholas the author of a detestable heresy among the deacons, it will be no wonder that the basest of men are found among the ranks of the saints.

—John Cassian, *Conference of Abbot Piamun*

Church growth

Do you not see that the more of them are executed, the more do the others grow in number?

—*Letter to Diognetus*

Like gold reduced in the furnace, it (the faith) has only been made to shine the more under the storms of persecution. . . .

—Theonas of Alexandria, *Epistle to Lucianus*

The Church of Christ has been founded by shedding its own blood not that of others. . . .

—Jerome, *Letter to Theophilus, Bishop of Alexandria*

Just as with the vine, when someone cuts away the fruit-bearing parts it grows up again and puts forth other branches both flourishing and fruitful—it happens in the same way with us.

—Justin Martyr, *Dialogue with Trypho the Jew*

We are but of yesterday, yet we have filled all that is yours; cities and islands, forts and towns, assemblies and even military camps, tribes, councils, the Palace, the Senate, the Forum. We left you only the temples.

—Tertullian, *Against the Jews XII*

The martyrs were bound, imprisoned, scourged, racked, burnt, rent, butchered—and they multiplied.

—Augustine

The more we are hewn down by you, the more numerous do we become.

—Tertullian, *Apology*

The blood of the martyrs is the seed of the Church.

—Jerome

An alien

The Church of God that lives as an alien in Rome to the Church of God that lives as an alien in Corinth. . . .

—Clement, *First Letter to the Corinthians*

Chain of command?

Let the laity be subject to the deacons; the deacons to the presbyters; the presbyters to the bishop; the bishop to Christ, even as he is to the Father.

—Ignatius, *Epistle to the Smyrnaeans*

Do I really need the Church?

. . . You would receive unity which you do not have, you would receive peace which you do not have. But if you regard these things as nothing, then fight, you deserter, fight against your commander who says, "He that gathereth not with Me, scattereth." Fight, then, against His apostle, yes, even against Him who speaks through him when he says, "Supporting one another in charity, careful to keep the unity of the Spirit in the bond of peace."

—Augustine, *The Lord's Prayer Explained*

Clothes, Cosmetics, Jewelry, etc.

As, then, in the fashioning of our clothes, we must keep clear of all strangeness, so in the use of them we must beware of extravagance.

—Clement of Alexandria, *The Instructor*

Simplicity provides for sanctity.

—Clement of Alexandria, *The Instructor*

Clothe yourselves with the silk of honesty, the fine linen of righteousness, and the purple of chastity. Thus painted you will have God for your lover.

—Tertullian, *On Female Dress*

The covering ought, in my judgment, to show that which is covered to be better than itself, as the image is superior to the temple, the soul to the body, and the body to the clothes.

—Clement of Alexandria, *The Instructor*

Love of display is not for a lady, but a courtesan.

—Clement of Alexandria, *The Instructor*

For as the brand shows the slave, so do gaudy colours the adulteress.

—Clement of Alexandria, *The Instructor*

In dress avoid sombre colours as much as bright ones. Showiness and slovenliness are alike to be shunned.

—Jerome, *Letter to Nepotian*

Cosmetics

Beauty fades, and falls quicker than the leaf on the ground, when the amorous storms of lust blow on it before the coming of autumn, and is withered by destruction.

—Clement of Alexandria, *The Instructor*

Is it not monstrous, that while horses, birds and the rest of the animals . . . rejoice in ornament that is their own, in mane, and natural colour, and varied plumage; woman, as if inferior to the brute creation, should think herself so unlovely as to need foreign, and bought, and painted beauty?

—Clement of Alexandria, *The Instructor*

But though they doctor the hair cleverly, they will not escape wrinkles, nor will they elude death by tricking time.

—Clement of Alexandria, *The Instructor*

The women who ought to scandalize Christians are those who paint their eyes and lips with rouge and cosmetics; whose chalked faces unnaturally white, are like idols; upon whose cheeks every chance tear leaves a furrow; who fail to realize that years make them old; who heap their heads with hair not their own; who smooth their faces, and rub out the wrinkles of age; and who, in the presence of their grandsons, behave like trembling schoolgirls.

—Jerome, *Letter to Paula*

With what confidence can a woman raise features to heaven which her Creator must fail to recognize?

—Jerome, *Letter to Furia*

Ornaments

How much more useful to acquire decorous friends, than lifeless ornaments!

—Clement of Alexandria, *The Instructor*

In the soul alone are beauty and deformity shown.

—Clement of Alexandria, *The Instructor*

Female habit carries with it a twofold idea—dress and ornament. By "dress" we mean what they call "womanly gracing," by "ornament" what is suitable should be called "womanly disgracing."

—Tertullian, *On the Apparel of Woman*

If one thinks himself made beautiful by gold, he is inferior to gold.

—Clement of Alexandria, *The Instructor*

I will give you a hint of what features to hide if you want to look your best. Show no nose upon your face and keep your mouth shut. You will then stand some chance of being counted both handsome and eloquent.

—Jerome, *Letter to Marcella*

What passes beyond the bounds of absurdity, is that they have invented mirrors for this artificial shape of theirs, as if it were some excellent work or masterpiece. The deception rather requires a veil thrown over it.

—Clement of Alexandria, *The Instructor*

Avoid men, also, when you see them loaded with chains and wearing their hair long like women, contrary to the apostle's precept.

—Jerome, *Letter to Eustochium*

Wigs?

Additions of other people's hair are entirely to be rejected, and it is a most sacrilegious thing for spurious hair to shade the head, covering the skull with dead locks. For on whom does the presbyter lay his hand? Whom does he bless? Not the woman decked out, but another's hair, and through them another head.

—Clement of Alexandria, *The Instructor*

The more old age strives to conceal itself, the more it will be detected. This, then, is your idea of true eternity, hair that is ever young! This is the incorruptibility which we have to put on for the new house of the Lord, one guaranteed by cosmetics!

—Tertullian, *On Female Dress*

If you feel no shame at the enormity, feel some at the pollution; for fear you may be fitting on a holy and Christian head the slough of someone else's head, unclean perchance, guilty perchance, and destined to hell.

—Tertullian, *On Female Dress*

⇼ Word to the wise

To Christian modesty it is not enough to *be* so, but to *seem* so, too. For so great ought its plenitude to be, that it may flow out from the mind to the garb, and burst out from the conscience to the outward appearance; so that even from the outside it may gaze, as it were, upon its own furniture.

—Tertullian, *On Female Dress*

In amplifying His law God makes no distinction of penalty between lust and fornication, and it will scarcely be that they escape punishment who have been to another the cause of perdition. That other, as soon as he has lusted after your beauty and in his mind committed the lustful act, perishes; and you have been made the sword of his destruction.

—Tertullian, *On Female Dress*

⇼ N.B.

The less you trouble to please other men, the more you will please them.

—Tertullian, *On Female Dress*

Commitment

Family ties

The love of God and the fear of hell will easily break such bonds.

—Jerome, *Letter to Heliodorus*

Total Commitment

Remember the day on which you enlisted, when, buried with Christ in baptism, you swore fealty to Him, declaring that for His sake you would spare neither father nor mother. Lo, the enemy is striving to slay Christ in you breast. Lo, the ranks of the foe sigh over that bounty which you received when you entered His service. Should your little nephew hang on your neck, pay no regard to him; should your mother with ashes on her hair and garments rent show you the breasts at which she nursed you, heed her not; should your father prostrate himself on the threshold, trample him under foot and go your way. With dry eyes fly to the standard of the cross. In such cases cruelty is the only true affection.

—Jerome, *Letter to Heliodorus*

Condemnation

Every sinner is inexcusable, be he a sinner by original guilt or by an additional guilt of his own will, whether he knows or not, whether he judges or not; for ignorance itself in those who do not want to know is without doubt a sin, and in those who are unable to know it is the penalty of sin. In neither case, then, is there a just excuse; but in both cases there is just condemnation.

—Augustine, *Letter to Sixtus*

We know that it is by a just judgment that it (mercy) is not given to those to whom it is not given at all.

—Augustine, *Letter to Vitalis, layman of Carthage*

Confession

No one lost Christ by confessing Him.

—Augustine, *The City of God*

Confession is not always confession of sins, but the praise of God is poured forth in the devotion of confession. The former mourneth, the latter rejoiceth: the former showeth the wound to the physician, the latter giveth thanks for health.

—Augustine, *Psalms*

Therefore, while it abases the man, it raises him; while it covers him with squalor, it renders him more clean; while it accuses, it excuses; while it condemns, it absolves. The less quarter you give yourself, the more (believe me) will God give you.

—Tertullian, *On Repentance*

There is no confession in the place of the departed. . . .

—Cyprian, *Epistles*

It grieves them (evil men) more to own a bad house than a bad life, as if it were man's greatest good to have everything good but himself.

—Augustine, *The City of God*

Confession of sin merits the remission of sin. For if we precede the devil in making our accusation, he will not be able to accuse us. If we become our own accusers, it profits us unto salvation.

—Origen, *Homilies on Leviticus*

(You) were not ashamed to sin but now are ashamed to confess.

—Pacian of Barcelona, *Sermon Exhorting to Penance*

When Peter denied the Son of God, he wept bitterly and effaced his threefold denial by a threefold confession.

—Jerome, *Letter to Marcella*

To Whom?

The same rationale is observed in the declaring of one's sins as in the detection of physical diseases. Just as the diseases of the body are not divulged to all, nor haphazardly, but to those who are skilled in curing them, so too our declaration of our sins.

—Basil the Great, *Rules Briefly Treated*

Be careful and circumspect in regard to whom you would confess your sins. Test first the physician to whom you would expose the cause of your illness.

—Origen, *Homilies on the Psalms*

He does not require that we come forward publicly to tell out our faults. He but commands us to make our explanation to Him alone, and to confess to Him. . . . He both forgives the sin and does not require that it be paraded before an audience. One thing only does He seek: that the person enjoying this forgiveness learn the greatness of the gift he has received.

—John Chrysostom, *Baptismal Catecheses*

Do you confess them to a fellow-servant, such as might make them public? No, you expose your wound to the Master, to the Guardian, to the Benefactor of mankind, to the Physician. . . .

—John Chrysostom, *Homilies Against the Anomoians*

. . . after confession his peril is greater, because the adversary is more provoked.

Cyprian, *Treatises.*

N.B.

Do not put it (sin) behind you, or God will put it in front of you.

—Augustine, *Sermons*

Contemplation

(See also: Meditation)

The active versus the contemplative life?

The active life is the journeying; the contemplative is the summit. The former makes a man holy; the latter makes him perfect. It is characteristic of the active life to inflict injuries on no one; of the contemplative, to bear inflicted injuries calmly. Nay, to state this more precisely, one who fulfills the requirements of the active life is prompt to forgive the man who has sinned against him; one who follows the contemplative life is prepared rather not to notice than to pardon the offenses. . . . The former controls anger by the virtue of patience; places the bridle of moderation on unrestrained passions; is touched by carnal desire but does not consent . . . is shaken by the attacks of the Devil but is not overcome. . . . The follower of the contemplative life by holy virtues overcomes all the feelings which variously affect the life of mortals; free from all desires and disturbances, he enjoys blessed quiet; and, being made superior to his temptations and passions by reason of his untrammeled mind he is raised on high by the indescribable joy of divine contemplation.

—Julian Pomerius, *The Contemplative Life*

At the summit of pure prayer, two states can be distinguished, one for the active, one for the contemplative. The first is the soul, the effect of the fear of God, and of good hope; and the second, of the fervor of divine love and of total purification. Indications of the first state: the spirit collects itself and abstracts itself from all thought of the world. . . . Indication of the second: the spirit, in the very upsurge of prayer, is ravished by the infinite light of God.

—Maximus, *The Centuries on Charity*

It is those who are perfect and purified from all faults who ought to seek the desert, and when they have thoroughly exterminated all their faults amid the assembly of the brethren, they should enter it not by way of cowardly flight, but for the purpose of divine contemplation, and with the desire of deeper insight into heavenly things, which can only be gained in solitude. . . .

—John Cassian, *The Institutes*

If a man knows not God, and knows not the things of God, he knows not "what things" he "has need of": for the things which he thinks he "has need of" are entirely wrong. On the other hand, he who contemplates what higher and holier things he lacks, will attain to objects of his contemplation, which are known by God and have been known to the Father or ever the request was made.

—Origen, *On Prayer*

Counselling

All wounds are not healed by the same medicine.

—Ignatius, *Letter to Polycarp*

Mitigate violent attacks by gentle applications.

—Ignatius, *Letter to Polycarp*

Courage

For if ye are silent concerning me, I shall become God's; but if ye show your love to my flesh, I shall again have to run my race. Pray, then, do not seek to confer any greater favour upon me than that I be sacrificed to God, while the altar is still prepared.

—Ignatius, *Epistle to the Romans*

Allow me to imitate the suffering of my God.

—Ignatius, *Epistle to the Romans*

Since our thoughts are not fixed on the present, we are not concerned when men cut us off; since also death is a debt which must at all events be paid.

—Justin, *The First Apology*

For a Christian body is not very greatly terrified at clubs, seeing all its hope is in the Wood. . . .

—Cyprian, *Epistles*

He who is near me is near the fire.

—Origen, *Homily on Jeremiah*

It is as a prisoner for Jesus Christ that I hope to greet you. . . . May I have the good fortune to meet my fate without interference.

—Ignatius, *Letter to the Romans*

You threaten me with the fire that burns for an hour and is speedily quenched; for you know nothing of the fire of the judgment to come.

—Polycarp, at his trial

The higher ground

We know many of our own number who have had themselves imprisoned in order to ransom others. Many have sold themselves into slavery and given the price to feed others.

—Clement, *First Letter to the Church in Corinth*

Stand firm, as does an anvil which is beaten.

—Ignatius, *Epistle to Polycarp*

Christ's soldier marches on through good report. . . . No praise elates him, no reproaches crush him. He is not puffed up by riches, nor does he shrink into himself because of poverty.

—Jerome, *Letter to Nepotian*

Is the world against Athanasius? Then Athanasius is against the world.

—Athanasius, at the Council of Nicea

Covetousness

. . . a secondary idolatry.

—Gregory of Nazianzus, *Orations on the Holy Lights*

He (Judas) could never have been impelled to this heinous sin of the betrayal if he had not been contaminated by the sin of covetousness; nor would he have made himself wickedly guilty of betraying the Lord, unless he had first accustomed himself to rob the bag entrusted to him.

—John Cassian, *Of the Spirit of Covetousness*

He (Judas) was ready no longer secretly to rob the bag, but actually to sell the Lord Himself.

—John Cassian, *Of the Spirit of Covetousness*

For it is possible even for one who has no money to be by no means free from the malady of covetousness, and for the blessing of penury to do him no good, because he has not been able to root out the sin of cupidity. . . .

—John Cassian, *Of the Spirit of Covetousness*

It is not the care for his children that makes a man covetous, but a disease of the soul.

—John Chrysostom, *Homilies on Thessalonians*

Creation

A witness

Two teachers, then, are given you from the beginning: creation and conscience. Neither of them has a voice to speak out; yet they teach men in silence.

—John Chrysostom, *Homilies on Hannah*

He did something that was better able to draw them to Him than a voice: He put creation in front of them so that the wise and the simple, the Scythian and the barbarian, having learned by vision the beauty of what they saw, might mount up to God.

—John Chrysostom, *Homilies on the Epistle to the Romans*

I asked the world about my God and it answered to me: "I am not He, but He made me."

—Augustine, *Confessions*

Others construct the whole fabric of the universe by chance accidents and by random collision, and fashion it by the concourse of atoms of the different shapes; with whom we by no means intend to enter . . . on a discussion of such perverse convictions . . . to argue against things palpably foolish, is a mark of greater folly.

—Arnobius, *Against the Heathen*

Some people read books in order to find God. Yet there is a great book, the very appearance of created things. Look above you; look below you! Note it; read it! God, whom you wish to find, never wrote that book with ink. Instead, He set before your eyes the things that He had made. Can you ask for a louder voice than that? Why, heaven and earth cry out to you: "God made me!"

—Augustine, *Sermon*

Creator . . . creation?

I refuse to adore the workmanship which He made for our sakes. The sun and moon were made for us; how, then, can I adore my own servant?

—Tatian, *Address to the Greeks*

Interrogate creation. If it is of itself, dwell in it. If, however, it is from Him, it is pernicious to one who loves it on this account alone, that it is preferred to the Creator.

—Augustine, *Confessions*

Nature cannot resist the Lord of nature.

—Jerome, *Letter to Vitalis*

God's speciality

God having made the quadrupeds, and wild beasts, and the land reptiles, pronounced no blessing upon them, reserving His blessing for man.

—Theophilus of Antioch, *To Autolycus*

⇹ Blueprint?

For man, being below, begins to build from the earth, and cannot in order make the roof, unless he has first laid the foundation. But the power of God is shown in this, that, first of all, He creates out of nothing . . . also . . . the creation of the heavens first of all took place, as a kind of roof saying: "At first God created the heavens" . . . and by "earth" he means the ground and foundation.

—Theophilus of Antioch, *To Autolycus*

Let us suppose that the existence of the universe is spontaneous. To what will you ascribe its preservation and its being maintained in the terms of its first existence? Something else, or is that also spontaneous? Surely to something other than chance! But what else can this be, except God?

—Gregory of Nazianzus, *Second Theological Oration*

⇹ Of Adam's rib

God had formed into a wife for him out of his rib. And this He did, not as if He were unable to make his wife separately, but God foreknew that man would call upon a number of gods. And having this prescience . . . lest then, it should be supposed that one God made the man and another woman, therefore He made them both; and God made the woman together with the man, not only that thus the mystery of God's sole government might be exhibited, but also that their mutual affection might be greater.

—Theophilus of Antioch, *To Autolycus*

⇹ N.B.

On the first day God made what He made out of nothing. But on the other days He did not make out of nothing, but out of what He had made on the first day, by molding it according to His pleasure.

—Hippolytus, *Commentary on Genesis*

Creed, Doctrine, Theology

Creed?

. . . a great amount of matter in a few words, and often, for the better understanding, designating an old article of the faith by the characteristic of a new name.

—Vincent of Lerins, *A Commonitory*

We are compelled to attempt what is unattainable, to climb where we cannot reach, to speak what we cannot utter. Instead of the bare adoration of faith, we are compelled to entrust the deep things of religion to the perils of human expression.

—Hilary of Poitiers

Theology

This divine initiator makes our divinized accents clearly sing the grandeurs of God. . . .

—Diodicus, *One Hundred Chapters on Spiritual Perfection*

(Theology) disposes us to despise happily all this life's friendships, by giving us the idea of replacing earthly desires with the ineffable riches of the Word of God.

—Diodicus, *One Hundred Chapters on Spiritual Perfection*

Back to the source

It is evident that all doctrine which agrees with those apostolic churches, the wombs and origins of the faith, must be reckoned for truth, as undoubtedly containing what the churches received from the apostles, the apostles from Christ, Christ from God.

—Tertullian, *The Rule of Faith*

In the Catholic Church itself, all possible care must be taken, that we hold that faith which has been believed everywhere, always, by all.

—Vincent of Lerins, *A Commonitory*

The Church of Christ, zealous and cautious of the dogmas deposited with it, never changes any phase of them. It does not diminish them or add to them; it neither trims what seems necessary nor grafts things superfluous.

—Vincent of Lerins, *A Commonitory*

Update?

It is right that those ancient doctrines of heavenly philosophy should, as time goes on, be cared for, smoothed, polished; but not that they should be changed, not that they should be maimed, not that they should be mutilated.

—Vincent of Lerins, *A Commonitory*

"Keep the Deposit"

What is "The Deposit?" That which has been instructed to thee, not that which thou hast thyself devised . . . a matter brought to thee, not put forth by thee.

—Vincent of Lerins, *A Commonitory*

Priority to creed

You did not first learn the Lord's Prayer and after that the Creed; but first the Creed, from which you should know what to believe, and afterward the Lord's Prayer, from which you should know whom to invoke. The Creed outlines the articles of faith, whereas the Lord's Prayer tells you how to address your petitions; because it is the man of faith that has his prayers heard.

—Augustine, *The Lord's Prayer Explained*

N.B.

And sometimes even they deny their own dogmas, when these are confuted, being ashamed openly to own what in private they glory in teaching.

—Clement of Alexandria, *The Stromata*

Cross

The wonderous Cross

Nature trembled and said with astonishment: What new mystery is this? The Judge is judged and remains silent; The invisible One is seen and does not hide Himself; The incomprehensible One is comprehended and does not resist; The unmeasurable One is measured and does not struggle; The One beyond suffering suffers and does not avenge Himself; The immortal dies and does not refuse death. What new mystery is this?

—Melito of Sardis, *Homily on the Passion*

All kings when they die have their power extinguished with their life: but Christ crucified is worshipped by the whole world. We proclaim The Crucified, and the devils tremble. . . .

—Cyril of Jerusalem, *Catechetical Lectures*

Well done, O Cross, that has cast off the ruler, brought home the robber, and called the apostle to repentance, and has not thought it beneath thy dignity to accept us.

—*Acts of Andrew*

If they were cast out of paradise because of the tree and the eating thereof, shall not believers now enter more easily into paradise because of the tree of Jesus?

—Cyril of Jerusalem, *Catechetical Lectures*

The sun was darkened, because of the Sun of Righteousness. Rocks were rent, because of the spiritual Rock. Tombs were opened, and the dead arose, because of Him who was free among the dead.

—Cyril of Jerusalem, *Catechetical Lectures*

The Plan

It was necessary, then, that one of two things should happen: either that God, in His truth, should destroy all men, or that in His loving-kindness He should blot out the sentence. But behold the wisdom of God: He preserved both the truth of His sentence, and the exercise of His loving-kindness. Christ bore our sins in His body on the tree. . . .

—Cyril of Jerusalem, *Catechetical Lectures*

Since it was through a tree that we lost the Logos in Paradise, it was through a tree again that the Logos was made manifest to all when He showed in Himself the length, the height, the depth, and the breadth, and as one of the oldest Christians said, He gathered together the two people to one God by stretching out both His hands.

—Ireneus, *Against Heresies*

The Power

If any disbelieve the power of the Crucified, let him ask the devils; if any believe not words, let him believe what he sees. Many have been crucified throughout the world, but by none of these are the devils scared; but when they see even the Sign of the Cross of Christ, who was crucified for us, they shudder.

—Cyril of Jerusalem, *Lecture on the Words, Crucified and Buried*

Adam by the tree fell away; thou by the Tree art brought into Paradise.

—Cyril of Jerusalem, *Lecture on the Word, Crucified and Buried*

N.B.

He is raised upon a high cross. . . . Who was He? Painful it is to tell, more terrible not to tell.

—Melito of Sardis, *Homily on the Passion*

Witness to the cross

Deny not the Crucified; for, if thou deny Him, thou hast many to arraign thee. Judas the traitor will arraign thee first; for he who betrayed Him knows that He was condemned to death by the chief-priests and elders. The thirty pieces of silver bear witness; Gethsemane bears witness, where the betrayal occurred; I speak not yet of the Mount of Olives, on which they were with Him at night, praying. The moon in the night bears witness; the day bears witness, and the sun which was darkened; for it endured not to look on the crime of the conspirators. The fire will arraign thee, by which Peter stood and warmed himself; if thou deny the Cross, the eternal fire awaits thee. I speak hard words, that thou may not experience hard pains. . . . The house of Caiaphas will arraign thee, shewing by its present desolation the power of Him who was erewhile judged there. Yea, Caiaphas himself will rise up against thee in the day of judgment. The very servant will rise up against thee, who smote Jesus with the palm of his hand; they also who bound Him, and they who led Him away. Even Herod shall rise up against thee; and Pilate; as if saying, Why deniest thou Him who was slandered before us by the Jews, and whom we knew to have done no wrong? . . . The false witnesses shall rise up against thee, and the soldiers who arrayed Him in the purple robe, and set on Him the crown of thorns, and crucified Him in Golgotha, and cast lots for His coat. . . .

From among the stars they will cry out upon thee, the darkened Sun; among the things upon earth, the Wine mingled with myrrh; among reeds, the Reed; among herbs, the Hyssop; among the things of the sea, the Sponge; among trees, the Wood of the Cross. . . .

—Cyril of Jerusalem, *Catechetical Lectures*

D

Death

Does it matter which kind?

And of what consequence is it what kind of death puts an end to life, since he who has died once is not forced to go through the same ordeal a second time?

—Augustine, *The City of God*

That death is not to be judged an evil which is the end of a good life; for death becomes evil only by the retribution which follows it. They, then, who are destined to die, need not be careful to inquire what death they are to die, but into what place death will usher them.

—Augustine, *The City of God*

The real villain

The death of our body is not inflicted on us by the law of nature, in which God made no death for man, but that it is inflicted as the deserts of sin.

—Augustine, *The City of God*

If we meditate on the fact that God did not make death, but only after man fell into the disgrace of guilt and deception did

God decree the sentence that earth should return to earth, we shall discover that death is the end of sin; and if we were to live longer our guilt would only be the greater.

—Ambrose of Milan, *Death as a Blessing*

We were not created to die, but we die by our own fault.

—Tatian, *Address to the Greeks*

The race is on

Our whole life is nothing but a race towards death, in which no one is allowed to stand still for a little space, or to go somewhat more slowly, but all are driven forward with an impartial movement, and with equal rapidity.

—Augustine, *City of God*

Death begins at birth.

—Gregory of Nyssa, *Virginity*

As soon as man is born he begins to sicken; he only terminates his sickness by his death.

—Augustine, *City of God*

Reflect well

Reflect upon the end of each of the preceding kings, how they died the death common to all, which, if it issued in insensibility, would be a godsend to all the wicked. But since sensation remains to all who have ever lived, and eternal punishment is laid up (i.e. for the wicked), see that ye neglect not to be convinced, and to hold as your belief, that these things are true.

—Justin, *The First Apology*

He is not worthy to receive consolation in death who has not reflected that he was about to die.

—Cyprian, *Epistles*

Live well, that ye may not die ill.

—Augustine, *Sermons on New Testament Lessons*

As a servant of God, thou oughtest even in death to please Him. Alas that the lifeless body should be adorned in death! A mind enchained to the world; not even in death devoted to Christ.

—Commodianus, *Instructions*

Therefore, since there is certainty as to the resurrection of the dead, grief on account of death is empty, as empty also is impatience in grief.

—Tertullian, *Patience*

Self-inflicted death?

For Judas, when he killed himself, killed a wicked man; but he passed from this life chargeable not only with the death of Christ, but with his own: for though he killed himself on account of his crime, his killing himself was another crime.

—Augustine, *The City of God*

The law, rightly interpreted even prohibits suicide, where it says, "Thou shalt not kill." This is proved specially by the omission of the words, "thy neighbor," which are inserted when false witness is forbidden.

—Augustine, *The City of God*

It is not without significance, that in no passage of the holy, canonical books there can be found either divine precept or permission to take away your own life.

—Augustine, *The City of God*

Christ's favorite term

For where resurrection had already taken place, He mentions

death with plainness; but where the resurrection is still a matter of hope, He says sleep. . . .

—John Chrysostom

This we affirm, this we maintain, this we every way pronounce to be right, that no man ought to inflict on himself voluntary death, for this is to escape the ills of time by plunging into those of eternity.

—Augustine, *The City of God*

N.B.

That which you think is death is only a departure.

—Tertullian, *Patience*

Death of Christ

For whom did He die?

If you are an unbeliever when you die, Christ did not die for you.

—Ambrose of Milan

I seek and I find that Christ Jesus died for all, except for God.

—Origen, *On the Soul*

Despise not a soul for whom Christ died!

—Jerome, *Letter to Pope Damasus*

Let us believe that the Son of God could not suffer, except for our sake.

—Barnabas, *Letter*

Why did He die?

Not one reason but many. First, that He might have dominion

over the living and the dead. Second, so that, by being sacrificed for us and by becoming a cursed thing on our behalf, He might wipe away our sins. Third, so that He might be offered to the God of all on behalf of the whole world. Fourth, so that He might Himself, with secret words, bring about the destruction of the demoniacal workings which lead so many astray. The fifth is this: so that holding out to His acquaintances and disciples the hope of life with God after death . . . He might bring on to completion those already more willing and those of greater courage; and so that with His rejection He might proclaim a religious polity to all, to Greeks and barbarians alike.

—Eusebius, *Proof of the Gospel*

Your money redeems you from the first death; the blood of your Lord redeems you from the second death.

—Augustine, *Sermons*

The Son of God is crucified; and I am not ashamed that it ought be cause for shame.

—Tertullian, *The Flesh of Christ*

By His own death putting death to death. . . .

—Epiphanius, *The Man Well-Anchored*

He who once conquered death on our behalf, always conquers it in us.

—Cyprian, *Epistles*

Adam received the sentence, *"Cursed is the ground in thy labors; thorns and thistles shall it bring forth to thee."* For this cause Jesus assumes the thorns, that He may cancel the sentence; for this cause also was He buried in the earth, that the earth which had been cursed might receive the blessing instead of a curse.

—Cyril of Jerusalem, *Catechetical Lectures*

The warders of hell trembled when they saw Him; and the gates of brass and the bolts of iron were broken. For, lo, the Only-begotten entered, a soul among souls. . . .

—Hippolytus, *Commentary on Matthew*

⇹ Why a public death?

Why, then . . . if it were necessary for Him to yield up His body to death in the stead of all, did He not lay it aside as man privately? . . .

Because the death which befalls men come to them agreeably to the weakness of their nature; for unable to continue in one stay, they are dissolved with time. . . . But the Lord is not weak, but is the Power of God and Word of God and Very Life. If, then, He had laid aside His body somewhere in private, and upon a bed, after the manner of men, it would have been thought that He also did this agreeably to the weakness of His nature, and because there was nothing in Him more than in other men.

—Athanasius, *Incarnation of the Word*

⇹ The form

Through the extension of His hands He gathered together the two peoples to the one God. There are two hands because there are two peoples scattered to the ends of the earth. And there is one Head in the middle as there is but one God who is above all and through all and in us all.

—Ireneus, *Against Heresies*

And it was a paradox, that the same one who was suffering was not suffering. He was suffering, in as much as His own body suffered, and He was in this suffering body; but He was not suffering, because the Word, being by nature God, is not subject to suffering.

—Athanasius, *Letter to Epictetus*

Body, soul, and spirit?

At the Passion they were separated. How? The body in the tomb, the soul in hell; the spirit, He commended it into His Father's hands.

—Origen, *On the Soul*

Why did God not prevent it all?

Since it was not fit that the Lord should fall sick, who healed the diseases of others. . . . Why, then, did He not prevent death, as He did sickness? Because it was for this that He had the body, and it was unfitting to prevent, lest the Resurrection also should be hindered, while yet it was equally unfitting for sickness to precede His death, lest His should be thought weakness on the part of the Him that was in the body.

—Athanasius, *Incarnation of the Word*

The scenario

An earthquake shook the world, the sea was heaved up from its depths, the heaven was shrouded in darkness, the sun's fiery blaze was checked, and his heat became moderate; for what else could occur when He was discovered to be God who heretofore was reckoned one of us?

—Arnobius, *Against the Heathen*

Demons

The nature of the demons has no place for repentance.

—Tatian, *Address to the Greeks*

Why are they here?

It has pleased the Lord of lords Himself in the heavens, that demons should wander in the world for our discipline.

—Commodianus, *Instructions*

Depravity

Unless we are assisted from above it is not possible for us to do right at any time.

—John Chrysostom, *Homilies on Genesis*

Camouflage

They tell of the attacks upon themselves of an evil spirit; their moral weaknesses they impute to fate or the stars. What they recognize as evil they do not want to acknowledge as their own.

—Tertullian

Devil

Tactics

Avoid the envenomed tongue of the devil, who from the beginning of the world . . . lies that he may deceive, cajoles that he may injure, promises good that he may give evil, promises life that he may put to death.

—Cyprian, *Epistles*

The enemy is more to be feared and to be guarded against, when he creeps on us secretly; when, deceiving by the appearance of peace, he steals forward by hidden approaches, whence also he has received the name of the Serpent.

—Cyprian, *On the Unity of the Church*

And herein lies the crafty cunning of our adversary, namely, in the fact that, where he cannot overcome the soldier of Christ by the weapons of the foe, he lays him low by his own spear.

—John Cassian, *Of the Spirit of Vainglory*

For Christ's adversary does not persecute and attack any except Christ's camp and soldiers; heretics, once prostrated and made his own, he despises and passes by. He seeks to cast down those whom he sees to stand.

—Cyprian, *Epistle to Lucius, the Bishop of Rome*

Before the advent of the Lord, the devil did not so plainly know the measure of his own punishment, in as much as the divine prophets had but enigmatically announced it. . . . But when the Lord appeared, and the devil clearly understood that eternal fire was laid up and prepared for him and his angels, he then began to plot without ceasing against the faithful, being desirous to have many companions in his apostasy, that he might not by himself endure the shame of condemnation, comforting himself by this cold and malicous consolation.

—Justin (quoted by John of Antioch)

Three secrets hidden from him

Mary's virginity and her giving birth escaped the notice of the prince of this world, as did the Lord's death—those three secrets crying to be told, but wrought in God's silence.

—Ignatius, *Letter to the Ephesians*

Why is his destruction delayed?

The reason why God has delayed to do this, is His regard for the human race. For He foreknows that some are to be saved by repentance, some even that are perhaps not yet born.

—Justin, *The First Apology*

He (God) suffered him to live, for two purposes, that he might disgrace himself the more in his defeat, and that mankind might be crowned with victory. . . . And that when victory was gained, he might be the more disgraced as being conquered by the weaker, and men be greatly honoured as having conquered him who was once an Archangel.

—Cyril of Jerusalem, *Lecture VIII*

Limited power

The adversary can do nothing against us except God shall have previously permitted it.

—Cyprian, *Treatises*

N.B.

For the Lord dwells in long-suffering, but the devil in anger.

—Hermas, *The Shepherd*

Discipline

Discipline is an index to doctrine.

—Tertullian

What benefits the body is called medicine; what benefits the soul, discipline.

—Augustine, *Moral Behavior of the Catholic Church*

Guideline

Where the crime committed was such that he who committed it is separated from the body of Christ, it is not so much the length of time as the depth of sorrow that is to be considered.

—Augustine, *Enchiridion of Faith, Hope and Love*

Discipline hath preceded; pardon also shall follow.

—Cyprian, *Epistles*

N.B.

Discipline, then, as far as we can gather from the sacred Scriptures, includes two things, restraint and instruction. Restraint implies fear, and instruction love. . . .

—Augustine, *Moral Behavior of the Catholic Church*

Divorce

Are there biblical grounds?

When a Christian husband has become unacceptable to a wife and she gives him the choice of separation from her or from Christ . . . the advice of the apostle is our guide. If the unbeliever refuses to remain with a believing spouse, let the believer recognize that he is free; let him not regard himself as in servitude so as to give up even the faith rather than to lose an unbelieving spouse.

—Augustine, *Letter to the Sicilian layman Hilary*

He is an adulterer, who married a woman divorced from her husband, or who divorced a wife on account of any crime except adultery. . . .

—Lactantius, *The Divine Institutions*

For if the law grants the freedom of giving notice of dismissal through an authoritative document, now evangelic faith enjoins upon a husband not only a good will in respect to keeping peace, but even levels against him a charge of collusion in regard to the adultery of a wife, if she marry another out of the necessity created by her separation; and it sets forth no other cause for terminating a marital union except this: lest a man might be soiled by the company of a promiscous wife.

—Hilary of Poitiers, *Commentary on the Gospel of Matthew*

If He conditionally forbade the dismissing of a wife, He did not forbid it absolutely; and what He did not forbid absolutely, He permitted in certain cases.

—Tertullian, *Against Marcion*

The man who withholds himself from his wife, often times makes her an adulteress, when he does not satisfy her desires, even though he withholds himself under the appearance of greater gravity and self-control. And perhaps this man who, so far as it rests with him, makes her an adulteress by not satisfying her desires, is more culpable than one who has divorced his wife for reasons other than fornication.

—Origen, *Commentaries on Matthew*

Nor is it allowed for one spouse to be separated from the other except for cause of fornication.

—Augustine, *Marriage and Concupiscene*

The Lord's declaration about the prohibition of departing from a marriage except for the reason of fornication, consistent with its meaning, applies equally to men and to women.

—Basil the Great, *Letter to Amphilochius, Bishop of Iconium*

"But if an unbeliever departs, let him depart." He protects the design of religion by his prior assertion that Christains may not forsake their spouses.

—Ambrose of Milan, *Commentaries on Thirteen Pauline Epistles*

For there is one thing which is commanded, another respecting which advice is given, another still which is allowed. A wife is commanded not to depart from her husband; and if she departs, to remain unmarried, or to be reconciled to her husband: therefore it is not allowable for her to act otherwise. But a believing husband is advised, if he has an unbelieving wife who is pleased to dwell with him, not to put her away: therefore it is allowable to put her away, because it is no command of the Lord that he should not put her away, but an advice of the apostle.

—Augustine, *Our Lord's Sermon on the Mount*

If an unbeliever departs out of hatred for God, the believer will not be guilty of having dissolved the marriage; for the honor of God is greater than that of matrimony. . . . There is no reverence owed to a marriage with a person who had a horror for the Author of marriage.

—Ambrose of Milan, *Commentaries on Thirteen Pauline Epistles*

Drink

It is exceedingly disgraceful that . . . wine should overpower him whom the sword assails in vain.

—Augustine, *To Publicola*

For if He made water wine at the marriage, He did not give permission to get drunk.

—Clement of Alexandria, *The Instructor*

I place no limit to a drunkard; but I prefer a beast.

—Commodianus, *Instructions*

It is proper, therefore, that boys and girls should keep as much as possible away from this medicine (wine). For it is not right to pour into the burning season of life the hottest of all liquids—wine—adding, as it were, fire to fire.

—Clement of Alexandria, *The Instructor*

"Use a little wine," says the apostle to Timothy, who drank water, "for thy stomach's sake"; most properly applying its aid as a strengthening tonic suitable to a sickly body . . . and specifying "a little," lest the remedy should, on account of its quantity, unobserved, create the necessity of other treatment.

—Clement of Alexandria, *The Instructor*

Let your breath never smell of wine lest the philosopher's words be said to you: "Instead of offering me a kiss you are giving me a taste of wine."

—Jerome, *Letter to Nepotian*

Priests given to wine are both condemned by the apostle and forbidden by the old law.

—Jerome, *Letter to Nepotian*

It was the custom of women to kiss their relatives, that they might be detected by their breath.

—Tertullian, *Apology*

He that lives in pleasure is dead while he lives, and he that drinks himself drunk is not only dead but buried.

—Jerome, *Letter to Oceanus*

One hour's debauch makes Noah uncover his nakedness which through sixty years of sobriety he had kept covered.

—Jerome, *Letter to Oceanus*

Lot in a fit of intoxication unwittingly adds incest to incontinence, and wine overcomes the man whom Sodom failed to conquer.

—Jerome, *Letter to Oceanus*

To many, total abstinence is easier than perfect moderation.

—Augustine, *On the Good of Marriage*

N.B.

The natural, temperate, and necessary beverage, therefore, for the thirsty is water.

—Clement of Alexandria, *The Instructor*

Election

Eternal purposes

It was not because we did believe, but so that we might believe, that He chose us.

—Augustine, *Predestination of the Saints*

For the term predestination does not express some compulsory necessity of the human will, but it foretells the eternal disposition, merciful and just, of a future divine operation.

—Fulgence of Ruspe, *To Monimus*

Man is not converted because he wills to be, but he wills to be because he is ordained to election.

—Augustine, *Predestination of the Saints*

Thou didst seek us when we sought Thee not; didst seek us indeed that we might seek Thee.

—Augustine, *Confessions*

God . . . does not bring to perfection of deed anyone whom He has not prepared beforehand in His eternal and unchangeable will.

—Fulgence of Ruspe, *Letters*

"He wills all men to be saved," is to be understood in reference to all the predestined.

—Augustine, *Admonition and Grace*

The apostles did not say: "He chose us before the foundation of the world, since we were holy and without blemish," but rather: "He chose us that we should be whole and without blemish."

—Jerome, *The Apology Against the Books of Rufinus*

Great is the mystery

We must admit that human understanding is unable to fathom the depths of God's judgments and we ought not to inquire why He who wishes all men to be saved does not in fact save all.

—Prosper of Aquitaine, *The Call of All Nations*

No one comes unless he is drawn. He draws one, and another He does not draw. Do not try to judge why He draws one and does not draw another, if you do not wish to err.

—Augustine, *Homilies on John*

Against my will?

Nor shall he who is saved be saved against his will.

—Clement of Alexandria, *The Stromata*

A man is able to come into the church unwillingly, he is able to approach the altar unwillingly, he is able to receive the Sacrament unwillingly; but he is not able to believe except willingly.

—Augustine, *Homilies on John*

"How do I believe willingly, if I am drawn?" I tell you: It is not so much that you are drawn by will as by pleasure . . . not by obligation, but by delight.

—Augustine, *Homilies on John*

Just as we speak correctly of some teacher of literature who is the only one in the city, when we say of him: "He teaches literature here to everyone," not because all learn, but because all who do learn literature there learn from him; so too we rightly say: "God teaches all to come to Christ," not because all do come, but because no one comes in any other way. . . .

—Augustine, *Predestination of the Saints*

"No man can come to Me unless the Father, who sent Me, draw him." Someone will say, "If a man come to Him, what need is there of drawing?" But this does not take away our faculty of choice, but only shows our need of help, because it points out that not just anyone may come at random, but he may come who is amply supplied with assistance.

—John Chrysostom, *Homilies on the Gospel of John*

Double election?

Neither did He predestine the wicked to the losing of righteousness as He predestined the saints to receiving of that same righteousness. . . .

—Fulgence of Ruspe, *To Monimus*

Those . . . whom He predestined to punishment, He did not predestine to guilt.

—Fulgence of Ruspe, *To Monimus*

But those who do not belong to His number of the predestined . . . are judged most justly according to their desserts. For either they lie under sin which they contracted originally by their generation and go forth with that hereditary debt which was not forgiven by regeneration, or they have added others besides through free choice: choice, I say, and free; but not freed. . . .

—Augustine, *Admonition and Grace*

Equality

Of the sexes

Their laws are unequal and irregular. Why did they restrain the woman but indulge the man? A woman who practices evil against her husband's bed is guilty of adultery, and for this the penalities of the law are very severe; but a husband committing fornication against his wife, has he no account to give? I do not accept this legislation nor do I approve this custom. . . . This is not how God acts. He says, "Honor thy father and thy mother."

—Gregory of Nazianzus, *On the Words of the Gospel in Matthew*

Eschatology

(See also: Prophecy, Second Coming)

Order of events?

In connection with the (Last) Judgment the following events shall come to pass, as we have learned: Elias the Tishbite shall come; the Jews shall believe; the Antichrist shall persecute; Christ will judge; the dead shall rise; the good and the wicked shall be separated; the world shall be burned and renewed. All these things we believe shall come to pass; but how, or in what order, human understanding cannot perfectly teach us, but only the experience of the events themselves. My opinion, however, is that they will happen in the order in which I have related them.

—Augustine, *The City of God*

And then will appear the signs of the truth. First, the sign spread out in the heavens; second, the sign of the sound of the trumpet; and third, the resurrection of the dead. . . . Then the world will see the Lord coming out on the clouds of heaven.

—Didache

The prophets have proclaimed His two comings. One, indeed, which has already taken place, was that of a dishonored and suffering Man. The second will take place when, in accord with prophecy, He shall come from the heavens in glory with His angelic host; when He shall raise the bodies of all the men who ever lived. Then He will clothe the worthy in immortality; but the wicked, clothed in eternal sensibility, He will commit to the eternal fire, along with the evil demons.

—Justin Martyr, *First Apology*

The two deaths

The first death drives the soul from the body against her will; the second death holds the soul in the body against her will.

—Augustine, *The City of God*

The two categories

To one group He designates a Kingdom, to the other, damnation in company with the Devil. There is no one left for a middle place. . . . Some will be on the right hand, others will be on the left hand: another hand I never knew.

—Augustine, *Sermons*

NB

For the end is always like the beginning.

—Origen, *De Principiis*

Eternity

There is nothing there that is past, as if it were no longer; nothing there is future, as if it not yet were. There is nothing there except "is."

—Augustine, *Psalms*

There day does not pass away to return with the year's rotation, but continues without sunset because it did not begin with sunrise.

—Augustine, *Sermon on Christmas*

Evangelism

We know that we, who already believe, act in upright faith when we pray for those who do not want to believe, that they may will to believe.

—Augustine, *Letter to Vitalis, layman of Carthage*

(If anyone) fail to talk about Jesus Christ, they are to me tombstones and graves of the dead.

—Ignatius of Antioch

Evil

Evil . . . nothing else than corruption.

—Augustine, *The Nature of the Good*

Example

Never either in you nor in her father let her see what she cannot imitate without sin.

—Jerome, *Letter to Laeta*

Sometimes the tone of the mistress is inferred from the dress of the maid.

—Jerome, *Letter to Furia*

Excess

All excess is foolish and futile for the servants of God.

—Hermas, *The Shepherd*

We must also check excessive laughter and immoderate tears.

—Clement of Alexandria, *The Instructor*

The possession and use of necessaries has nothing injurious in quality, but it has in quality above measure.

—Clement of Alexandria, *Maximus, Sermon 13*

Just as an excess of sadness plunges the soul into despair and lack of faith, so excess of joy invites it to presumption.

—Diodicus, *One Hundred Chapters on Spiritual Perfection*

To the weak and infirm, what is moderate appears excessive.

—Clement of Alexandria, *Sermon on the Lazy and Indolent*

Excessive grief

Although the death of sons leaves grief for the heart, yet it is not right either to go forth in black garments, or to bewail them. The Lord prudently says that ye must grieve with the mind, not with outward show, which is finished in the week.

—Commodianus, *Instructions*

Excessive affection

Too great affection towards one's children is disaffection towards God.

—Jerome, *Letter to Paula*

A tumour though it enlarges the size of the body is injurious to health.

—Jerome, *Letter to Tranquillinus*

N.B.

Let her meals always leave her hungry. . . .

—Jerome, *Letter to Laeta*

Faith

Definitions

Faith is to believe what we do not see, and the reward of this faith is to see what we believe.

—Augustine

Faith is the ear of the soul.

—Clement of Alexandria, *The Stromata*

Faith is the greatest mother of the virtues.

—Clement of Alexandria, *The Stromata*

For since faith is one and the same, he who can say much about it does not add to it, nor does he who can say little diminish it.

—Athenagoras, *A Plea Regarding Christians*

Faith and reason?

If we were to judge everything according to our intellect, and to decide that which our mind cannot comprehend is impossible, gone is faith. . . .

—Basil of Caesarea, *Against Eunomius*

Believe, so that you may understand.

—Augustine, *Sermons*

God does not expect us to submit our faith to Him without reason, but the very limits of our reason make faith a necessity.

—Augustine

It is reasonably demanded that faith precede reason.

—Augustine, *Letter to Consentius*

It is good that faith should precede reason, lest we seem to demand reasons from our Lord God in the same way that we might demand them of a man.

—Ambrose of Milan, *Abraham*

There are three kinds of credible things. First there are those which are always believed and never understood. An example of such is all history. . . . Second, there are those things which first are understood, so that they can be believed. Of this class are all human reasonings. . . . The third class is of those things which are believed first and understood afterwards. Of such kind as this are the aspects of divine things which cannot be understood except by those who are pure in heart.

—Augustine, *Eighty-Three Diverse Questions*

Faith and works

It is therefore of no advantage to them after the end of life, even if they do good works now, if they have no faith.

—Clement of Alexandria, *The Epistle to the Corinthians*

We are justified not by our own works, but by faith.

—Clement of Rome, *First Epistle to the Corinthians*

Without faith every human labor is empty.

—Fulgence of Ruspe, *The Rule of Faith*

Neither faith without works nor works without faith is of any avail.

—Gregory the Great, *Homilies on Ezekiel*

Do not doubt whether it is possible: for He that on this sacred Golgotha saved the robber after only one hour of believing, the same will save you, if you believe.

—Cyril of Jerusalem, *Catechetical Lectures*

Its glorious absurdity

God's Son died: It is believable precisely because it is absurd. . . . He was buried and rose again: It is certain because it is impossible.

—Tertullian

Faith and godliness

Faith and godliness . . . are so closely allied that they can be considered sisters.

—Athanasius, *Resurrection Letter IX*

Gift of God

"But what do you have that you did not receive . . . ?" It was chiefly by this testimony that I myself too was converted, when I likewise erred, thinking that the faith by which we believe in God is not a gift of God, but is in us for ourselves. . . .

—Augustine, *Predestination of the Saints*

To be able to have faith, just as to be able to have love, belongs to men by nature; but actually to have faith, as also actually to have love, belongs to the faithful by grace.

—Augustine, *Predestination of the Saints*

The work of faith is not ours, "It is the gift," he says, "of God."

—John Chrysostome, *Homilies on the Epistle to the Ephesians*

To persevere in faith is certainly a gift from God. . . .

—Hilary of Poitiers, *Commentaries on the Psalms*

Progress in faith?

If faith itself could not be led to its perfection through various degrees, certainly the Holy Apostles would never have said: "Increase our faith."

—Gregory the Great, *Homilies on Ezekiel*

Faith will lead you in; experience will teach you; Scripture will train you. . . .

—Clement of Alexandria, *Exhortation to the Heathen*

Faith plus nothing

What is it that has saved you? Your hoping in God alone, and your having faith in Him in regard to what He promised and did give. Beyond this there is nothing that you have contributed.

—John Chrysostom, *Homilies on the Epistle to the Romans*

Its universality

In the Catholic Church itself, all possible care must be taken, that we hold that faith which has been believed everywhere, always, by all.

—Vincent of Lerins, *A Commonitory*

Its urgency

No soul whatever is able to obtain salvation, unless it has believed while it was in the flesh.

—Tertullian, *The Resurrection of the Dead*

For nothing is done for the love of God unless first there be belief in God.

—Augustine, *Psalms*

What of Old Testament saints?

Christ was shown to holy men of old, that they might be saved by faith in His passion to come, just as we are saved by faith in His passion already past.

—Augustine, *Confessions*

N.B.

Faith fears no famine.

—Tertullian

For it is not the same thing to believe **in** a thing and to believe **about** it.

—Gregory of Nazianzus, *On the Holy Spirit*

The disbelief of Thomas has done more for our faith than the faith of the other disciples.

—Gregory the Great

Falsehood

It is an old saying, "Liars are disbelieved even when they speak the truth."

—Jerome, *Letter to Eustochium*

It is beyond all doubt, worse to swear falsely by the true God than to swear truly by the false gods.

—Augustine, *To Publicola*

Never will I consent to conceal my beliefs, nor shall my opinions be at war with my tongue.

—Synesius, to his brother

To speak evil of the righteous is a sin not easily pardoned.

—Jerome, *Letter to Asella*

For the sin of the man who tells a lie to help another is not so heinous as that of the man who tells a lie to injure another.

—Augustine, *Enchiridion*

For there is a difference between lying and being a liar. A man may tell a lie unwillingly; but a liar loves to lie, and inhabits in his mind the delight of lying.

—Augustine, *On Lying*

Since then by lying eternal life is lost, never for any man's temporal life must a lie be told.

—Augustine, *On Lying*

Degrees of falsehood

Every lie is a sin, though it makes a great difference with what intention and on what subject one lies. For the sin of the man who tells a lie to help another is not so heinous as that of the man who tells a lie to injure another; and the man who by his lying puts a traveller on the wrong road, does not do so much harm as the man who by false or misleading representations distorts the whole course of a life.

—Augustine, *Enchiridion*

Many lies are apparently told out of kindness, not malice, the object being someone's safety or advantage; such were the lies told by the midwives in Exodus who gave a false report to Pharaoh in order to save the male infants of Israel from death. But even here what is praiseworthy is not the action but the motive, since those who merely tell lies such as theirs will deserve in time to be set free from all dissimulation, for in the perfect not even these are to be found.

—Augustine, *Psalms*

There are two kinds of lies which are no great crime but not exactly free from sin, the lie spoken in jest, and the lie spoken to render some service.

—Augustine, *Psalms*

Fasting

Fasting . . . the escorting attendant of their prayers.

—Tertullian, *On Fasting*

(Adam) yielded more readily to his belly than to God, heeded the meat rather than the mandate, and sold salvation for his gullet!

—Tertullian, *On Fasting*

Fasting was her recreation and her refreshment.

—Jerome, *Letter to Marcella*

Distinctives

I recognize, therefore, *animal* faith by its care of the flesh. . . .

—Tertullian, *On Fasting*

Directives

Lay upon yourself only as much fasting as you can bear, and let your fasts be pure, chaste, simple, moderate, and not superstitious.

—Jerome, *Letter to Nepotian*

Don't fast by the mouth, but also by the eye, the ear, the feet, the hands—all members of your body. Let your hands fast by being pure from stealing. . . . Let your feet fast by not running to watch things you shouldn't. Let your eyes fast, being taught not to look at things they shouldn't, and especially not to stare at beautiful women. . . . Let the ear fast . . . in refusing to listen to evil talk and rumours. . . . Let the mouth, too, fast from disgraceful talk.

—Chrysostom, *Sermons*

The strictest fast is bread and water.

—Jerome, *Letter to Nepotian*

When I am in Rome, I fast on Saturday; but here I do not. If you do not want to scandalize or be scandalized, follow the custom of whatever church you attend.

—Ambrose, quoted by Augustine in his letter to Januarius

A meager diet which leaves the appetite always unsatisfied is to be preferred to fast three days long. It is much better to take a little every day than some days to abstain wholly and on others to surfeit oneself. That rain is best which falls slowly to the ground. Showers that come down suddenly and with violence wash away the soil.

—Jerome, *Letter to Furia*

Let your fast be of daily occurrence and your refreshment such as avoids satiety. It is idle to carry an empty stomach if, in two or three days' time, the fast is to be made up for by repletion.

—Jerome, *Letter to Eustochium*

Raison d'etre

Fast, because fasting will train your body for martydom, your skin will be strengthened to bear the iron nails; when your blood is well-nigh exhausted you will bleed the less beneath the scourge.

—Tertullian, *On Fasting*

He prescribed to fasts a law—that they are to be performed "without sadness": for why should what is salutary be sad? He taught likewise that fasts are to be the weapons for battling with the more direful demons: for what wonder if the same operation is the instrument of the iniquitous spirit's egress as of the Holy Spirit's ingress?

—Tertullian, *On Fasting*

N.B.

When the stomach is full, it is easy to talk of fasting.

—Jerome, *Letter to Paulinus*

An over-fed Christian will be more necessary to bears and lions, perchance, than to God.

—Tertullian, *On Fasting*

Flattery

Flattery is the bane of friendship. Most men are accustomed to pay court to the good fortune of princes, rather than to the princes themselves.

—Clement of Alexandria, *Sermon 2, John of Damascus*

Flee from wheedling flatterers as from open enemies.

—Jerome, *Letter to Paulinus*

Food

We are enjoined to reign and rule over meats, not to be slaves to them.

—Clement of Alexandria, *The Instructor*

Meat kills as many as the musket; the board as the sword.

—John Chrysostom

About the measure of abstinence in food and drink, the fathers say that one should partake of the one and the other in a measure somewhat less than one's actual need.

—Barsanuphius, *Directions in Spiritual Work*

Let her meals always leave her hungry. . . .

—Jerome, *Letter to Laeta*

Foreknowledge

God foreknows all the things of which He is the Author. But He is not Himself the Author of all that He foreknows. He is not the evil author of what He is the Just Avenger.

—Augustine, *Free Choice*

Man . . . does not sin because God foreknew that he would sin.

—Augustine, *The City of God*

Just as you do not, by your memory of them, compel past events to have happened, neither does God, by His foreknowledge, compel future events to take place.

—Augustine, *Free Choice*

Nor can it be doubted that it is man himself who sins, when he does sin, because He whose foreknowledge cannot err foreknew that it was not fate, nor fortune, nor something else, but man himself who was going to sin.

—Augustine, *The City of God*

We must recognize that while God foreknows all things, He does not predestine all things. He foreknows the things that depend on us, but He does not predestine those things. He does not will the doing of evil, nor does He compel virtue.

—John Damascene, *The Source of Knowledge*

Ask Him why He chose the traitor Judas; why He committed the coffers to him when He knew that Judas was a thief. Do you want to hear the reason? God judges the present, not the future.

—Jerome, *Dialogue Against the Pelagians*

It is not because God knew the future that Adam sinned; but God foreknew, as God, that Adam would do this of his own will.

—Jerome, *Dialogue Against the Pelagians*

He foretold and promised a reward for the enjoyment of the righteous; He did not promise, however, but only foretold a torment for the punishment of the unrighteous.

—Fulgence of Ruspe, *To Monimus*

Forgiveness

Not perfect, but pardoned

I will not glory because I am righteous, but because I am redeemed; not because I am clear of sin, but because my sins are forgiven.

—Ambrose of Milan

Complete

The sins committed before faith are accordingly forgiven by the

Lord, not that they may be undone, but as if they had not been done.

—Clement of Alexandria, *The Stromata*

N.B.

By denying forgiveness they remove the incentive to repentance.

—Ambrose of Milan, *Penance*

"Forgive us our trespasses, as we forgive those who trespass against us." What if God should answer. . . . Why do you ask me to do what I have promised, when you refuse to do what I have commanded?

—Augustine, *The Lord's Prayer Explained*

Free Will

Does it conflict with divine grace?

These two then; viz., the grace of God and free will seem opposed to each other, but really are in harmony.

—John Cassian, *The Third Conference of Abbot Chaeremon*

It does not follow that, though there is for God a certain order of all causes, there must therefore be nothing depending on the free exercise of our own wills, for our wills themselves are included in that order of causes which is certain to God, and is embraced by His foreknowledge.

—Augustine, *The City of God*

Neither is freedom of the will taken away because help is given. Rather, help is given because freedom is not taken away.

—Augustine, *Letter to the Sicilian layman Hilary*

And when His goodness sees in us even the very smallest spark of good-will shining forth, which He Himself has struck as it were out of the hard flints of our hearts, He fans and fosters it and nurses it with His breath, as He "willeth all men to be saved."

—John Cassian, *The Third Conference of Abbot Chaeremon*

Let us take care not to defend grace in such a way that we would seem to take away free choice; nor again can we insist so strongly on free choice that we could be judged, in our proud impiety, ungrateful for the grace of God.

—Augustine, *Forgiveness of Sins*

For if thou wert a fornicator by necessity, then for what cause did God prepare hell? If thou wert a doer of righteousness by nature and not by will, wherefore did God prepare crowns of ineffable glory? The sheep is gentle, but never was it crowned for its gentleness: since its gentle quality belongs to it not from choice but by nature.

—Cyril of Jerusalem, *Catechetical Lectures*

The choice of the will and the grace of God has such difficulty in its distinctions that when free choice is defended it seems to be a denial of God's grace and when God's grace is asserted free choice may seem to be taken away.

—Augustine, *Grace and Original Sin*

Limits?

If the way to truth is hidden from a man, free choice avails him nothing except for sinning.

—Augustine, *The Spirit and the Letter*

Without His help we neither will nor do anything good.

—Augustine, *Grace and Original Sin*

Our free-will has destroyed us; we who were free have become slaves.

—Tatian, *Address to the Greeks*

Man was lost by free will; the God-man came by a freeing grace.

—Augustine, *Sermons*

For, as a man who kills himself must, of course, be alive when he kills himself, but after he has killed himself ceases to live, and cannot restore himself to life; so, when man by his own free-will sinned, then sin being victorious over him, the freedom of his will was lost.

—Augustine, *Enchiridion*

For the Spirit of God who moves you, by so moving, is your Helper. The very term helper makes it clear that you yourself are doing something.

—Augustine, *Sermons*

Even the good use of free will . . . is from God.

—Augustine, *Revisions*

Free choice, therefore, suffices for evil, but is too little for good.

—Augustine, *Admonition and Grace*

We must consider diligently and carefully how these pairs differ among themselves: to be able not to sin, and not to be able to sin; to be able not to die, and not to be able to die; to be able not to forsake good, and not to be able to forsake good. For the first man was able not to sin, able not to die, able not to forsake good. . . . The first freedom of will, therefore, was to be able not to sin; but the last will be much greater, not to be able to sin.

—Augustine, *Admonition and Grace*

Attempted at reconciliation

God created us with free will, and we are not forced by necessity either to virtue or to vice. Otherwise, where there were necessity there would be no crown. Just as with good works, it is God who brings them to perfection, depending not so much on him that wills nor on him that runs as on God who pities and assists him to reach the goal.

—Jerome, *Against Jovinian*

You may perhaps say that a man is saved by God's mercy alone; and others will say that unless a man's own will accompanies and cooperates with that mercy, he will not be able to be saved. And both views may rightly be held, if a proper order of divine mercy and human will be observed, so that the one comes before and the other follows after. The beginning of salvation is conferred by God's mercy alone. With that mercy the human will then becomes the cooperatrix. In this way the mercy of God comes before and directs the course of the human will; and the human will, being obedient, follows after that same mercy. . . .

—Fulgence of Ruspe, *Letter to John and Venerius*

N.B.

You must not have a monopoly of bending the law to suit your will instead of bending your will to suit the law.

—Jerome, *Letter to Oceanus*

Objections to free will

"Therefore He hath mercy on whom He will, and whom He will He hardeneth."

Answer: It will not be superfluous to employ . . . an illustration, as if, e.g. one were to say that it is the sun which hardens and liquefies, although liquefying and hardening are things of an opposite nature. Now it is not incorrect to say that the sun, by one and the same power of its heat, melts wax indeed, but dries up and hardens mud: not that its power operates one way upon mud, and in another way upon wax; but that the qualities of mud and wax are different, although according to nature they are one thing, both being from the earth. In this way, then, one and the same working upon the part of God, which was administered by Moses in signs and wonders, made manifest the hardness of Pharaoh . . . but exhibited the obedience of those other Egyptians who were intermingled with the Israelites, and who are recorded to have quitted Egypt at the same time with the Hebrews.

—Origen, *De Principiis*

The sun also blinds those whose sight is dim: and they whose eyes are diseased are hurt by the light and blinded. Not that the sun's nature is to blind, but that the substance of the eyes is incapable of seeing. In like manner unbelievers being diseased in their heart cannot look upon the radiance of the Godhead.

—Cyril of Jerusalem, *Catechetical Lectures*

Friendship

A friend is long sought, hardly found, and with difficulty kept.

—Jerome, *Letter to Rufinus*

The friendship which can cease has never been real.

—Jerome, *Letter to Rufinus*

Never look a gift horse in the mouth.

—Jerome, *Epistle to the Ephesians*

God

First of all, believe that there is one God who created and finished all things, and made all things out of nothing. He alone is able to contain the whole, but Himself cannot be contained.

—The Shepherd of Hermas

What image of God can I invent since in reality man himself is God's image.

—Minucius Felix, *Octavius*

God, then, being not a subject for demonstration, cannot be the object of science.

—Clement of Alexandria, *The Stromata*

Omnipresent

He can be present unperceived, and be absent without moving.

—Augustine, *The City of God*

Therefore, thinking what He wills, and then willing what He thinks, He is all thought, all will, all mind, all light, all eye, all ear, all fountain of every good.

—Irenaeus, *Against Heresies*

God is an infinite circle whose circumference is nowhere.

—Augustine

He can in no way be contained in a place. If He were, the place containing Him would be greater than He is; for that which contains is greater than that which is contained.

—Theophilus of Antioch, *To Autolycus*

Omnipotent

But assuredly He is rightly called omnipotent, though He can neither die nor fall into error. For He is called omnipotent on account of His doing what He wills, not on account of His suffering what He wills not.

—Augustine, *The City of God*

To be able in one thing, and to be unable in another, is a word which cannot be said of God.

—Hippolytus, *Against Plato*

Whatever moves something is stronger than that which is moved, and whatever maintains something is stronger than that which is maintained. I call the One who constructed all things and maintains them *God*.

—Aristides of Athens, *Apology*

He cannot do some things for the very reason that He is omnipotent.

—Augustine, *The City of God*

Omniscient

Wretched that I am! I have not remembered that God observes the mind, and hears the voice of the soul.

—Peter of Alexandria, *Fragment*

He foreknoweth the things that shall be, and is mightier than all, knowing all things and doing as He will; not being subject to any necessary sequence of events, nor to nativity, nor chance, nor fate; in all things perfect, and equally possessing every absolute form of virtue, neither diminishing nor increasing, but in mode and conditions ever the same. . . .

—Cyril of Jerusalem, *Catechetical Lectures*

Invisible

Tell me what thoughts of God we should conceive? One, all things seeing, yet Himself unseen.

—Philemon, quoted by Justin

As, therefore, the seed of the pomegranate dwelling inside, cannot see what is outside the rind, itself being within; so neither can man who along with the whole creation is enclosed by the hand of God, behold God.

—Theophilus of Antioch, *To Autolycus*

Of all visible things, the world is the greatest; of all invisible, the greatest is God. But, that the world is, we can see; that God is, we believe.

—Augustine, *The City of God*

"Blessed are the pure in heart, for they shall see God." . . . What else is seeing God in heart, but, according to our exposition . . . understanding and knowing Him with the mind? . . . In all the Scriptures, both old and new, the term "heart" (is) repeatedly used of "mind," i.e. intellectual power.

—Origen, *De Principiis*

"Angels do always behold the face of My Father which is in heaven. . . ." Yes, but the angels see God as He is, but only as far as they themselves are capable.

—Cyril of Jerusalem, *Catechetical Lectures*

Eternal

Nor . . . is He apprehended by the science of demonstration. For it depends on primary and better known principles. There is nothing antecedent to the Unbegotten.

—Clement of Alexandria, *The Stromata*

God always was, and always will be. Or rather, God always is.

—Gregory of Nazianzus, *On the Theophany*

The world . . . cannot be coeternal with God. For every effect is later in origin and in time than the one effecting it.

—Zachary of Mitylene, *Disputation*

For all that is divine is liable neither to destruction nor to origination.

—Hilary of Poitiers, *The Trinity*

Of all beings that exist, who is without cause? The Godhead. None can tell the cause of God; else he were older than God.

—Gregory of Nazianzus, *Third Theological Oration*

He is always unbounded, because nothing is greater than He; always eternal, because nothing is more ancient than He. For that which is without beginning can be preceded by none, in that He has no time.

—Novatian, *Treatise Concerning the Trinity*

The Nameless One

To the Father of all, who is unbegotten, no name is given; for anyone who has been given a name has received the name from someone older than himself.

—Justin, *Second Apology*

The appellation "God" is not a name but the notion implanted in the nature of men of a thing which can hardly be explained.

—Justin, *Second Apology*

There is no one name sufficiently broad to take the whole nature of God.

—Basil the Great, *Against Eunomius*

I am of the opinion that Moses, when he asked: "What is Thy name?" wanted to know what is peculiar to God, and to know something special about Him. God, knowing what was on his mind, did not, therefore, tell him His name but His occupation. That is, He expresses a thing, not an appellative, when He says: "I am that I am": for there is nothing more peculiar to God than always to exist.

—Ambrose of Milan, *Commentaries on Twelve Psalms of David*

Self-revealing

Without God, God cannot be known.

—Irenaeus, *Against Heresies*

Whom shall we believe about God, more than God Himself.

—Ambrose of Milan, *Letter to the Emperor Vanentinium*

Father

There never was a time when God was not the Father.

—Dionysius the Great, *Refutation and Defense*

God's love of man is such that to those for whom first He is the Creator, He afterwards, according to grace, becomes a Father also.

—Athanasius, *Discourses Against the Arians*

I would rather sense these things about the Father than speak of them.

—Hilary of Poitiers, *The Trinity*

(He) had ever His paternity, if I may so speak, coextensively with His eternity.

—Basil the Great, *Against Eunomius*

Incomprehensible

If you comprehend, He is not God. Let there be a pious confession of ignorance rather than a rash profession of knowledge.

—Augustine, *Sermons*

He knows how to receive into Himself without Himself being increased thereby, just as He knows how to impart Himself in such a way as Himself, to suffer no loss.

—Leporius, *Letter to the Gallican Bishops*

It is not to be wondered at if Thou art unknown; it is a cause of greater astonishment if Thou art clearly comprehended.

—Arnobius, *Against the Heathen*

If the least of His works are incomprehensible, shall He be comprehended who made them all?

—Cyril of Jerusalem, *Catechetical Lectures*

In those matters which concern God, to confess our ignorance is already great knowledge.

—Cyril of Jerusalem, *Catechetical Lectures*

He is greater than mind itself; nor can it be conceived how great He is, seeing that if He could be conceived, He would be smaller than the human mind wherein He could be conceived.

—Novatian, *Treatise Concerning the Trinity*

⇚ Indescribable

We must believe in Him, we must apprehend Him, we must worship Him; and it is these acts which must stand in place of our describing Him.

—Hilary of Poitiers, *The Trinity*

God always was, and is, and will be; or better, He always is. *Was* and *will be* are portions of time as we reckon it, and are of a changing nature. He, however, is ever existing; and that is how He names Himself in treating with Moses on the mountain.

—Gregory of Nazianzus, *Second Oration on Easter*

⇚ Unbegotten

That which is from no one is without beginning; and what is without beginning is unbegotten.

—Basil the Great, *Against Eunomius*

Perfect Begetter of the perfect *Begotten,* Father of the only-begotten Son.

—Gregory Thautmaturgus, *A Declaration of Faith*

⇚ How great Thou art

In glory He is incomprehensible, in greatness unfathomable, in height inconceivable, in power incomparable, in wisdom unrivalled, in goodness inimitable, in kindness unutterable.

—Theophilus of Antioch, *To Autolycus*

He cannot be seen, for He is too bright for sight; nor can He be grasped, for He is too pure to touch; nor can He be measured, for He is too great for the senses.

—Minucius Felix, *Octavius*

He is Lord because He rules over all things; Father because He is before all things; Designer and Creator, because He is Maker and Creator of all things; Most High, because He is above everything; Almighty, because He Himself rules and encompasses all.

—Theophilus of Antioch, *To Autolycus*

He is without beginning, because He is unbegotten; and He is unchangeable, because He is immortal.

—Theophilus of Antioch, *To Autolycus*

The Father, having begotten the Son, remained Father, and did not become other than He was. He begot Wisdom, but did not Himself become unwise. He begot Power, and was not weakened. He begot God, but lost not His own divinity. He neither lost anything of Himself by diminution or change; nor is there anything lacking in Him that was begotten. He that begot is God; and God is He that was begotten.

—Cyril of Jerusalem, *Catechetical Lectures*

N.B.

Our God has no introduction in time. He alone is without beginning, and is Himself the beginning of all things.

—Tatian the Syrian, *Address to the Greeks*

What is not born cannot be changed.

—Novatian, *Treatise Concerning the Trinity*

Look for anything better if you can find it; God keeps Himself for you.

—Augustine, *On Psalms*

Goodness

Nothing is so mighty as sovereign good.

—Boethius, *The Consolation of Philosophy*

It must be understood that our wickednesses are entirely our own, but our goodnesses pertain both to the Almighty God and to ourselves.

—Gregory the Great, *Homilies on Ezekiel*

The good we do is both of God and of ourselves. It is God's through prevenient grace, ours through obedient free will. For if it is not God's, why do we give thanks to Him in eternity? And again, if it is not ours, why do we hope that a reward will be given us? It is not improper that we give thanks; for we know that we were anticipated by God's gift. And again, it is not improper that we seek a reward, because we know that by obedient free will we chose to do what is good.

—Gregory the Great, *Moral Teachings from Job*

But when good is done by the fear of penalty, not by the love of righteousness, good is not yet well done.

—Augustine, *Controversy with Pelagius*

You will not find that upright people have ever been disowned by holy men. The righteous, to be sure, have been persecuted, but by wicked men.

—Clement, *First Letter to the Church of Corinth*

Grace

What is grace? Something given *gratis*. What is given *gratis*? That which is bestowed rather than paid as owed.

—Augustine, *Homilies on John*

The grace of God does not find men fit for salvation, but makes them so.

—Augustine

Undeserved

That they become in birth vessels of wrath is due to a penalty deserved; but that in a rebirth they become vessels of mercy is due to grace undeserved.

—Augustine, *Letter to Optatus of Mauretania Tingitana*

There can be no doubt that all who actually come to the knowledge of the truth and to salvation do so not in virtue of their own merits but of the efficacious help of divine grace.

—Prosper of Aquitaine, *The Call to All Nations*

Nothing of human merit precedes the grace of God.

—Augustine, *Letter to Paulinus of Nola*

Beware, O Christian, beware of pride. For though thou art a follower of the saints, ascribe it always wholly to grace; for that there should be any "remnant" in thee, the grace of God hath brought to pass, not thine own desserts.

—Augustine, *Sermon on New Testament Lessons*

Oh, how great is the loving-kindness of God! On those who have defected from Him, and who were in the extremities of wickedness, He has bestowed such an amnesty for their wicked deeds and so great a sharing in grace that they may even call Him Father.

—Cyril of Jerusalem, *Catechetical Lectures*

What merits of his own has the saved to boast of when, if he were dealt with according to his merits, he would be nothing if not damned? Have the just then no merits at all? Of course they do, for they are the just. But they had no merits by which they were made just.

—Augustine, *Letter to Sixtus*

For the grace of God would not be grace in any way unless it were gratuitious in every way.

—Augustine, *Grace and Original Sin*

We plainly assert our unconditional opinion that the grace of God is superabounding, and sometimes overflows the narrow limits of man's lack of faith.

—John Cassian, *The Third Conferences of Abbot Chaeremon*

. . . man even though he strive with all his might for a good result, yet cannot become master of what is good unless he has acquired it simply by the gift of Divine bounty and not by the efforts of his own toil.

—John Cassian, *The Third Conference of Abbot Chaeremon*

We do not think that grace is given to anyone because of his own merits, nor do we suppose that anyone is punished except on his own desserts.

—Augustine, *Gift of Perseverance*

And whatever evils I have not done, that too I reckon as Your grace.

—Augustine, *Confessions*

Perfect balance

"For by grace," (Paul) says, "you have been saved." But lest the greatness of the benefits inflate you, see how he brings you down: "By grace you have been saved," he says, "through faith." And then again, lest a violence be done free will, after he has added what pertains to us he takes it away again when he says, "and that not of ourselves." The faith, he means, is not from ourselves; for if He had not come, if He had not called, how should we be able to believe?

—John Chrysostom, *Homilies on the Epistle to the Ephesians*

"If salvation is by grace," someone will say, "why is it that we are not all saved?" Because you did not will it; for grace, even though it be grace, saves the willing, not those who are not willing and who turn away from it and who constantly fight against it and oppose themselves to it.

—John Chrysostom, *Homilies on the Epistle to the Ephesians*

Just as a writing-pen or a dart has need of one to employ it, so also does grace have need of believing hearts. . . . It is God's part to confer grace, but yours to accept and guard it.

—Cyril of Jerusalem, *Catechetical Lectures*

He giveth more grace

It is not enough for me that God has given me grace once, but He must give it always. I ask, that I may receive; and when I have received, I ask again. I am covetous of receiving God's bounty. . . . The more I drink, the more thirsty I become.

—Jerome, *Letter to Ctesiphon*

Prevenient

"His mercy shall prevent me" (Psalms 59:10). Truly He forestalled you; He had to forestall you, because He found not an atom of virtue in you. You had forestalled His chastisement by your pride; He has forstalled your punishment by wiping out your sins.

—Augustine, *On Psalms*

The first gifts of grace are not like the last.

—Epiphanius, *Panarion*

N.B.

If you want to be cast forth from grace, brag about your merits.

—Augustine, *On Psalms*

Either let us fear the wrath to come or let us value the grace we have: one or the other.

—Ignatius, *Letter to the Ephesians*

Grief

Why do we grieve for the dead? We are not born to live forever.

—Jerome, *Letter to Paula*

You must regret him not as dead but as absent.

—Jerome, *Letter to Heliodorus*

We should indeed mourn for the dead, but only for him whom Gehenna receives.

—Jerome, *Letter to Paula*

Happiness

But what else is it to live happily, except to know that one has something eternally?

—Augustine, *Eighty-Three Diverse Questions*

Man wishes to be happy even when he lives so as to make happiness impossible.

—Augustine

Recipes

Happiness is found in the practice of virtue.

—Clement of Alexandria, *The Instructor*

Happy is he who makes daily progress and who considers not what he did yesterday, but what advance he can make today.

—Jerome

By whose gift all are happy who are happy through verity and not through vanity.

—Augustine, *The City of God*

Pleasure is the fruit of decent living.

—Lactantius Firmianus, *The Divine Institutes*

How that can be true happiness which has no assurance of lasting in eternity? . . .

—Augustine, *The City of God*

Happiness . . . is effected by the combination of two things, that is, both that it enjoy without any interruption the unchangeable good, which is God, and that it can be certain beyond any doubt . . . that it is to remain eternally in that same enjoyment.

—Augustine, *The City of God*

The highest degree of happiness is, not to sin; the second, to acknowledge our sins.

—Cyrian, *Epistles*

Whatever you possess on earth is inferior to yourself. . . . You want to be better off; I know it, we all know it, we all want the same thing. Look for what is better than yourself, so that by that means you may become better off than you are.

—Augustine, *On Psalms*

False happiness

The gain of a penny fills us with joy, the loss of a halfpenny, with sorrow.

—Jerome, *Letter to Marcella*

Unhappiness is the inseparable companion of wickedness.

—Augustine, *On Psalms*

N.B.

Happy are they who recognize their Father!

—Tertullian, *On Prayer*

Hatred

"Thou shalt hate thine enemy," . . . is not to be understood as the voice of command addressed to a righteous man, but rather as the voice of permission to a weak man.

—Augustine, *Our Lord's Sermon on the Mount*

Hatreds are accounted impious by martyrs for the flame.

—Commodianus, *Instructions*

Healing

We beseech Thee, Savior of all men, Thou that hast all virtue and power, Father of our Lord and Savior Jesus Christ, and we pray that thou wilt, from heaven, the healing power of the Only-begotten upon this oil, so that for those (who are anointed . . .), it may be effective for the casting out of every disease and every bodily infirmity, for an antidote against every demon, for escape from every unclean spirit, for the expulsion of every evil spirit, for the banishing of every fever and chill and every weakness, for good grace and remission of sins, for a remedy unto life and deliverance, for health and integrity of soul, of body, and of spirit, for perfect vigor.

—Serapion, *Prayer Over the Oil of the Sick or Over Water*

It is in many ways a grander virtue and a more splendid achievement to cure the weaknesses of one's own soul than those of the body of another.

—John Cassian, *The Second Conference of Abbot Nesteros*

Am I in health? I thank my Creator. Am I sick? In this case, too, I praise God's will.

—Jerome, *Letter to Paula*

Heaven

If one man should suffer all the sorrows of all the saints in the world, yet they are not worth one hour's glory in heaven.

—John Chrysostom

We shall live close to God and with God, our souls steadfast and free from passion. Even if we have flesh, it will not seem so: we shall have heavenly spirits.

—Athenagoras, *A Plea Regarding Christians*

As . . . the soul even now finds it impossible to desire unhappiness, so in future it shall be wholly impossible for it to desire sin.

—Augustine, *Enchiridion*

Hell

Some think that hell is a definite place on the earth, but others suppose that it is under the earth. It does seem to me, however, that if we call something infernal because it is situated in a lower position, then hell ought to be infernal to the earth, just as the earth is infernal to the heavens.

—Gregory the Great, *Dialogues*

He has prepared heaven, but He has also prepared hell.

—Letter to Cyprian from the Roman clergy

Nor is there either measure or end to these torments. That clever fire burns the limbs and restores them, wear them away and yet sustains them. Just as fiery thunderbolts strike bodies but do not consume them; just as the fires of Mount Etna and Mount Vesuvius and of burning lands everywhere blaze without being wasted; so also that fiery punishment is fed not by consuming those who burn, but is nourished by the unending eating away of their bodies.

—Minucius Felix, *Octavius*

The same divine fire . . . will both consume the wicked and recreate them; and as much as it takes away from their bodies, that much also will it replace, while it will be for itself its own supply of eternal food.

—Lactantius, *The Divine Institutions*

What can there be that is worse than hell? Yet nothing is more profitable than the fear of it!

—John Chrysostom, *Homilies on the Incident of the Statues*

If the soul sinned naked and alone, let it alone be punished; but if it has an evident accomplice, the just Judge will not dismiss that accomplice. I hear Scripture too saying that for the condemned just punishments are ordered: fire and darkness and a worm. All of these are punishments suited to composite and material bodies.

—Gregory of Nyssa, *On the Holy Pasch*

Let us see what is meant by the threatening with eternal fire. We find in the prophet Isaiah that the fire with which each one is punished is described as his own; for he says: "Walk in the light of your fire and in the flame which you have kindled for yourselves." It seems to be indicated by these words that every sinner kindles for himself the flame of his own fire and is not plunged into some fire which was kindled beforehand by someone else. . . . The food and fuel of this fire are our own sins, which are called wood and hay and stubble by the Apostle Paul.

—Origen, *De Principiis*

And the devil and his demons, and the man that is his, the Antichrist, and the impious and the sinners shall be consigned to everlasting fire, not material fire such as we know, but such fire as God would know.

—John Damascene, *The Source of Knowledge*

The Lord descended into the regions beneath the earth, announcing there the good news of His coming. . . .

—Irenaeus, *Against Heresies*

N.B.

If we always think of hell, we shall not soon fall into it.

—John Chrysostom, *Homilies on Thessalonians*

Heresy

The passion for ruling is the mother of heresy.

—John Chrysostom

It is evil mingling chalk in the milk of God.

—Quoted by Irenaeus, *Against Heresies*

There are three states of the soul—ignorance, opinion, knowledge—those who are in ignorance are the pagans (Gentiles), those in knowledge, the true Church, and those in opinion, the Heretics.

—Clement of Alexandria, *The Stromata*

I warn you in advance against wild beasts in human shapes.

—Ignatius, *Letter to the Smyraneans*

Manipulating the Scriptures

(Heretics) will not make use of all the Scriptures, and . . . they will not quote them entire, nor as the body and texture of prophecy prescribe. But, selecting ambiguous expressions, they wrest them to their own opinions, gathering a few expressions here and there; not looking to the sense, but making use of the mere words.

—Clement of Alexandria, *The Stromata*

In the Church of God the teacher's error is in the people's trial.

—Vincent of Lerins, *A Commonitory*

Let no license be allowed to novelty, because it is not fit that any addition should be made to antiquity. Let not the clear faith and belief of our forefathers be fouled by any muddy admixture.

—Sixtus II, *Epistle to the Bishop of Antioch*

For it is as bad an error to add to our Lord Jesus Christ what does not belong to Him as to rob Him of that which is His.

—John Cassian, *The Seven Books of John Cassian*

No one can be a better churchman than one who has never been a heretic.

—Jerome, *Letter to Theophilus, Bishop of Alexandria*

They do, in fact, what nurses do when they would prepare some bitter draught for children; they smear the edge of the cup all round with honey. . . .

—Vincent of Lerins, *A Commonitory*

And so one after another out of reaction against heresies they give rise to heresies, and all teach things different from each other, but equally opposed to the faith.

—John Cassian, *The Seven Books of John Cassian*

It is out of truth that falsehood is built; out of religion that superstition is compacted.

—Tertullian, *On Fasting*

Semi-heretics

They have . . . swallowed a quantity of poison—not enough to kill, yet more than can be got rid of; it neither causes death, nor suffers to live. O wretched condition!

—Vincent of Lerins, *A Commonitory*

We anathematize the Macedonians, who, coming as offspring of the Arians, have changed their name but not their faithlessness.

—Damasus, *The Tome of Damasus*

Heresy and schism?

Between heresy and schism there is this distinction to be made, that heresy involves perverse doctrine, while schism separates one from the Church on account of disagreement with the bishop.

—Jerome, *Commentaries on the Epistle to Titus*

Emulation of the episcopal office is the mother of schisms.

—Tertullian, *On Baptism*

Formerly the heretics were manifest, but now the Church is filled with heretics in disguise.

—Cyril of Jerusalem, *Lecture X*

Apocryphal writings

. . . they are not written by those to whom they are ascribed . . . many faulty elements have been introduced into them, and . . . it requires infinite discretion to look for gold in the midst of dirt.

—Jerome, *Letter to Laeta*

Increased danger

Formerly the heretics were manifest; but now the Church is filled with heretics in disguise.

—Cyril of Jerusalem, *Lecture XV*

Antidote

Let them unlearn well what they had learnt not well, and let them receive so much of the entire doctrine of the Church as they can understand: what they cannot understand let them believe.

—Vincent of Lerins, *A Commonitory*

In the Church itself regard must be had to the consentient voice of universality equally with that of antiquity, lest we either be torn from the integrity of unity and carried away to schism, or be precipitated from the religion of antiquity into heretical novelties.

—Vincent of Lerins, *A Commonitory*

It is the best thing never to fall into error: the second best thing to make a good repudiation of it.

—John Cassian, *The Seven Books of John Cassian*

N.B.

Use only Christian food. Keep off foreign fare, by which I mean heresy.

—Ignatius, *Learn to the Traillians*

Holiness

Only a holy servant can serve in holiness.

—Epiphanius, *Panarion*

They who restrain baser lusts, not by the power of the Holy Spirit . . . or by the love of intelligible beauty, but by desire of human praise . . . are not indeed yet holy, but only less base.

—Augustine, *The City of God*

Few of those who forsake error at the call of virtue can begin on the highest level, and after indulging themselves with everything, cut off all indulgence at one stroke.

—Apollinaris Sidonius, *Letter to Ambrose*

Holy kiss

Do not suppose that this kiss is like those given by mutual friends in the market-place. Such a kiss this is not. This kiss blends souls one with another, and woos for them forgetfulness of every injury. This kiss, then, is a sign of the intermingling of souls and of the banishment of every remembrance of injury. . . . This kiss, therefore, is reconciliation, and because of this it is holy.

—Cyril of Jerusalem, *Catechetical Lectures*

Holy Communion

The best guard for the preserving of a benefit is remembrance of that benefit, and perpetual thanksgiving.

—John Chrysostom, *Homilies of the Gospel of Matthew*

Three distinctives

The Sacraments, very few in number, very easy of observance, and most sublime in meaning.

—Augustine, *Letter to Januarius*

"Let a man examine . . ."

He does not command that one is to be examined by another, but each is to examine himself, making the courtroom secret and the trial unwitnessed.

—John Chrysostom, *Homilies on the First Epistle to the Corinthians*

This is the Body which He gave us both to hold in reserve and to eat, which was appropriate to intense love; for those whom we kiss with abandon we often even bite with our teeth.

—John Chrysostom, *Homilies on the First Epistle to the Corinthians*

We ought not to suspend ourselves from the Lord's Communion because we confess ourselves sinners, but should more and more eagerly hasten to it for the healing of our soul. . . .

—John Cassian, *Conference of Abbot Joseph*

Agape

The nature of our meal and its purpose are explained by its very name. It is called *Agape*, as the Greeks call love in its purest sense. However much it may cost, it is always a gain to be extravagant in the name of fellowship with what is God's, since the food brought is used for the benefit of all who are in need.

—Tertullian, *Apology*

What if the celebrant is unworthy?

All the Sacraments, while they are injurious to those who administer them unworthily, are beneficial to those who receive them unworthily.

—Augustine, *Against the Letter of Parmenian*

Just as Judas to whom the Lord handed a morsel, furnished in himself a place for the devil, not by receiving something wicked but by receiving it wickedly, so too anyone who receives the Sacrament of the Lord unworthily does not, because he himself is wicked, cause the Sacrament to be wicked.

—Augustine, *Baptism*

How can I conscientiously approach Christ's eucharist and answer the Amen if I doubt the charity of him who ministers it?

—Jerome, *Letter to Theophilus, Bishop of Alexandria*

N.B.

Contrary to the vigour of the Gospel, contrary to the law of the Lord and God, by the temerity of some, communion is relaxed to heedless persons—a vain and false peace, dangerous to those who grant it, and likely to avail nothing to those who receive it.

—Cyprian, *On the Unity of the Church*

Just as this bread which we break,
once scattered over the hills,
has been gathered and made one,
so may Thy Church too be assembled
from the ends of the earth into Thy Kingdom!
For glory and power are Thine forever.

—*Didache*

The Holy Spirit

The Spirit and the Godhead

The Son of God poured forth the gift He received from the Father: the Holy Spirit, third name of the Divinity, the third degree of Majesty, the Proclaimer of the one Rulership, the

Administrator of the various branches of the household.

—Tertullian, *Against Praxeas*

If He is given, if He is received, if He is retained, then obviously He exists.

—Hilary of Poitiers, *The Trinity*

If anyone does not say that the Holy Spirit is truly and properly of the Father, just as the Son, of the divine substance and true God: he is a heretic.

—Damasus, *The Tome of Damasus*

If ever there was a time when the Father was not, then there was a time when the Son was not. If ever there was a time when the Son was not, then there was a time when the Spirit was not. If the One was from the beginning, then the Three were so too.

—Gregory of Nazianzus, *Fifth Theological Oration*

We know that the Holy Spirit is the gift of God, the gift being Himself indeed equal to the Giver.

—Augustine, *Enchiridion*

He is the Gift of God, so we may believe that God does not give a Gift inferior to Himself.

—Augustine, *Faith and the Creed*

Not when man wishes the spirit to speak does the Holy Spirit speak, but it speaks only when God wishes it to speak.

—The Shepherd of Hermas

The Holy Spirit is truly holy. No other is such, not in the same way; for He is holy not by an acquiring of holiness but because He Himself is Holiness; not more holy at one time and less holy another time; for there is no beginning in time of His being holy, nor will there ever be an end of it.

—Gregory of Nazianzus, *In Praise of Hero the Philosopher*

The Lord Jesus Himself has not only, as God, given the Holy Spirit, but also, as Man, He has received Him.

—Augustine, *The Trinity*

Scripture speaks of "the Holy Spirit, who proceeds from the Father" who, since He proceeds from there, is not a creature; who, since He is between the Unbegotten and the Begotten, is God. . . . What then, is procession? Tell me first what is the unbegotteness of the Father, and then I will physiologize for you on the generation of the Son and the procession of the Spirit: and we will both be frenzy-stricken for prying into God's mysteries. . . .

—Gregory of Nazianzus, *Fifth Theological Oration*

For neither has the Son anything else except those things given Him by the Father, nor has the Holy Spirit any other substance than that given Him by the Son. . . . We believe that in the Trinity the nature of the Holy Spirit is the same as that of the Father and the Son.

—Didymus the Blind, *The Holy Spirit*

He is third in appellation, equal in divinity, not different as compared to Father and Son, connecting Bond of the Trinity, Ratifying Seal of the creed.

—Epiphanius, *Panacea Against All Heresies*

Who would dare to say that the Holy Spirit is separated from the Father and Christ, when it is through Him that we attain to the image and likeness of God, and through Him that . . . we become "partakers of the divine nature."

—Ambrose of Milan, *The Holy Spirit*

The Spirit and the believer

What the soul is to man's body, the Holy Spirit is to the Body of Christ, which is the Church.

—Augustine, *Sermons*

He said that all things should be taught us by the Spirit when He should come to dwell amongst us. Of these things one, I take it, was the Deity of the Spirit Himself.

—Gregory of Nazianzus, *On the Holy Spirit*

To live, then, is Christ; and to understand is the Spirit.

—Marius Victorinus, *Against Arius*

Know thou that every man is either empty or full. For if he has not the Holy Spirit, he has no knowledge of the Creator; he has not received Jesus Christ the life.

—Irenaeus, *Fragments from Lost Writings*

To each who receives the Spirit it is as if he alone received Him; yet the grace the Spirit pours out is quite sufficient for the whole of mankind. All who share in Him share not according to the measure of His power but according to the capacity of their own nature.

—Basil the Great, *The Holy Spirit*

Sin against the Holy Spirit

This sin is hardness of heart persisted into the end of this life. . . .

—Augustine, *Letter to Boniface, vicar of Africa*

The sin which shall never be forgiven is not the blasphemy of men disembowelled by torture who in their agony deny their Lord, but it is the captious clamour of those whom while they see that God's works are the fruit of virtue, ascribe the virtue to a demon and declare the signs wrought to belong not to the divine excellence but to the devil.

—Jerome, *Letter to Marcella*

This is perhaps the sin against the Holy Ghost, i.e. through malice and envy to act in opposition to brotherly love after receiving the grace of the Holy Ghost.

—Augustine, *Our Lord's Sermon on the Mount*

Homosexuality

All other frenzies of passions—impious both toward the bodies and toward the sexes—beyond the laws of nature, we banish not only from the threshold, but from all shelter of the Church, because they are not sins, but monstrosities.

—Tertullian, *On Modesty*

As far as sex is concerned, the Christian is content with the woman.

—Tertullian

To defilers of boys, communion is not to be given even at death.

—The Council of Elvira

Hope

What then is hope? Confidence in things to come.

—John Chrysostom, *Homilies on the Epistle to the Romans*

Hope . . . is compared to an egg. For hope has not yet arrived at attainment; and an egg is something, but not yet the chicken.

—Augustine, *Sermons on New Testament Lessons*

Despair belongs to the crass sluggard; hope, however, is an incentive to labor.

—Ambrose of Milan, *Commentary on Psalm 118*

There will no longer be hope, when the reality will be present.

—Augustine, *Sermons*

Hope has for its object only what is good, only what is future, and only what effects the man who entertains the hope.

—Augustine, *Enchiridion*

Humility

Humility is the root, mother, nurse, foundation and bond of all virtue.

—John Chrysostom

For those who would learn God's ways, humility is the first thing, humility is the second, humility is the third.

—Augustine

It was pride that changed angels into devils; it is humility that makes men as angels.

—Augustine

Humility . . . is the mistress of all virtues.

—John Cassian, *The Second Conference of Abbot Nesteros*

Paths of humility

When He has performed a good work, let him remember the evil he has done, that his contrition for his evil deeds may moderate his joy for his good works.

—Gregory the Great, *Pastoral Care*

Blushing for shame you will be dragged before the public. That is good for you, for he who is not publicly exposed like this before men will be publicly exposed before God.

—Tertullian, *On Flight in Persecution*

Give me strength to raise my head to a level with the saints' heels!

—Jerome, *Letter to Rufinus*

Do not wish to seem very devout nor more humble than need be, lest you seek glory by shunning it.

—Jerome, *Letter to Eustochium*

When he is exalted and appointed that he may be useful to others in the post which is offered him, he should avoid it in spirit, and yet out of obedience accept it.

—Gregory the Great, *Pastoral Care*

As it is not possible to go into battle naked, or to swim over a great sea fully clothed, or to live without breathing, so without humility and constant supplication to Christ, it is not possible to learn the secret war of the mind.

—Hesychius of Jerusalem, *Texts on Sobriety and Prayer*

Abbot Piamun after twenty-five years did not hesitate to receive some grapes and wine offered to him by a certain brother, and at once preferred, against his rule, to taste what was brought him rather than to display his abstinence which was a secret from everybody.

—John Cassian, *Second Conference of Abbot Piamun*

His refusal (of the priesthood) did but prove him worthy of an office which he was reluctant to assume, and all the more worthy because he declared himself unworthy.

—Jerome, *Letter to Heliodorus*

As pride was the beginning of sin, so humility must be the beginning of the Christian discipline.

—Augustine

The supreme example

When the disciples were apppointed to preach the Gospel they were told to take with them neither shoe nor shoe-latchet; and when the soldiers came to cast lots for the garments of Jesus they found no boots that they could take away. For the Lord could not Himself possess what He had forbidden to His servants.

—Jerome, *Letter to Eustochium*

He took upon Him, therefore, the form of man; and under the guise of our race He imprisoned His power, so that He could be seen and carefully regarded, might speak and teach, without encroaching on the sovereignty and government of the King Supreme. . . .

—Arnobius, *Against the Heathen*

N.B.

If we behave like lambs, we are victorious; even though ten thousand wolves should hem us in we survive and overcome. But if we turn ourselves into wolves, we are overcome; for the help of the shepherd is withdrawn from us. For He is the shepherd of sheep and not wolves.

—John Chrysostom, *Homilies on Matthew*

Hypocrisy

Some kissed my hands, yet attacked me with the tongues of vipers; sympathy was on their lips, but malignant joy in their hearts.

—Jerome, *Letter to Asella*

Why do we profess one thing, and practice another? The tongue talks of chastity, but the rest of the body reveals incontinence.

—Jerome, *Letter to Furia*

There is nothing great in wearing a sad or a disfigured face, in simulating and in showing off fasts, or in wearing a cheap cloak while you retain a large income.

—Jerome, *Letter to Paulinus*

He professes himself to be a Christian in such a way as the devil often feigns himself to be Christ.

—Cyprian, *Treatises*

I

Idleness

A man asleep is worth nothing, any more than if he were not alive.

—Clement of Alexandria, *The Instructor*

If the one coming to you is only a traveler, help him as much as you can, but he shall stay with you only for two days, if necessary three. If someone wants to settle among you, let him work in his trade for a living and in case he has no trade or craft, use your discretion and see to it that no idle Christian lives in your midst.

—*Didache*

Ignorance

It is idle to try to teach what you do not know, and—if I may speak with some warmth—it is worse still to be ignorant of your ignorance.

—Jerome, *Letter to Paulinus*

We shall not injure God by remaining ignorant of Him, but shall deprive ourselves of His friendship.

—Justin Martyr

It is better to avoid danger at the price of ignorance than to court it for the sake of learning.

—Jerome, *Letter to Eustochium*

Ignorance of Christ?

Of the Son it is said: "Of that day and hour no one knows, except the Father; not the angels in heaven and not the Son." . . . If God is one, how can there be a diversity of knowledge in one divinity? . . . If He is God, how does He not know? . . . In the Apostles we read about Christ: "In whom are hidden all the treasures of wisdom and knowledge." . . . Not that some are and some are not: but *all* the treasures of wisdom and knowledge; but they are *hidden*. So what is in Him is not lacking to Him, even though it be hidden from us.

—Jerome, *Homilies on the Gospel of Mark*

He does not know the day which He causes not to be known, not because He Himself does not know it, but because He does not permit it to be known at all.

—Gregory the Great, *Letter to Eulogius*

"Of that day and hour no one knows, neither the angels of heaven nor the Son, except the Father." By the saying, "Neither the angels," He stopped their mouths, lest they seek to learn what even the angels did not know: and by the saying, "nor the Son," He forbids them not only to learn but even to inquire. . . . He refers this knowledge to the Father both to make the matter more awesome and to preclude their inquiring about it.

—John Chrysostom, *Homilies on the Gospel of Matthew*

The Only-begotten, incarnate and made perfect Man for us, did indeed *in* His human nature know the day and the hour of the judgment, but nevertheless did not know this *from* His human nature. What He knew *in* it He did not on that account know *from* it.

—Gregory the Great, *Letter to Eulogius*

Incarnation

(See also: Nativity; Virgin Birth)

Great is the mystery

But of all the marvelous and mighty acts related to Him, this altogether surpasses human admiration . . . that the wisdom of God can have entered the womb of a woman, and have been born an infant, and have uttered wailings like cries of little children.

—Origen, *De Principiis*

He who shuts up the world in His fist is contained in the narrow limits of a manger.

—Jerome, *Letter to Eustochium*

In God there is one substance, but three Persons; in Christ two substances, but one Person.

—Vincent of Lerins, *A Commonitory*

Look for Christ, the Son of God; who was before time, yet appeared in time; who was invisible by nature; yet visible in the flesh; who was impalpable, and could not be touched, as being without a body but for our sakes become such, might be touched and handled in the body; who was impossible as God but became possible for our sakes as men.

—Ignatius, *Epistle to Polycarp*

We have not two Christs, not two royal Sons of God, but the same who is God, the same is Man; not as indwelling in man, but He is made whole Man. . . . "The Word became flesh." For he did not say, "The flesh became Word," so that he can show that the Word first came down from heaven, made the flesh from the womb of the holy Virgin subsist in Himself and reshaped the whole humanity perfectly into Himself.

—Epiphanius, *Panacea Against All Heresies*

"In the beginning was the Word": behold Him to whom Mary hearkened; "and the Word was made flesh": behold Him whom Martha served.

—Augustine

He who was born of the Holy Spirit is the Son of God the Father, not of the Holy Spirit.

—Augustine, *Enchiridion*

⇹ The raison d'etre

Christ became what we are that He might make us what He is.

—Athanasius, *Incarnation of the Word of God*

The Son wished to be sent and to become the Son of Man, so that he might make us the sons of God.

—Cyprian, *Works and Almsgiving*

Jesus Christ our Lord, who, on account of His great love, became what we are, so that He might bring us to what He Himself is.

—Irenaeus, *Against Heresies*

⇹ More reasons

If He had not appeared in the flesh, men could never have survived the sight of Him. They even have to shut their eyes when looking at the sun. . . .

—Barnabas, *A Letter*

Like as when a great king has entered into some large city and taken up his abode in one of the houses there, such city is at all events held worthy of honour, nor does any enemy or bandit any longer descend upon it and subject it; but, on the contrary, it is thought entitled to all care, because of the king's having taken up his residence in a single house there: so, too, has it been with the Monarch of all. For now that He has come to our realm, and taken up His abode in one body among His peers, henceforth the whole conspiracy of the enemy against mankind is checked, and the corruption of death which before was prevailing against them is done away. For the race of men had gone to ruin, had not the Lord and Saviour of all, the Son of God, come among us to meet the end of death.

—Athanasius, *Incarnation of the Word*

God saw that mankind, worship things created; He put on a created body, that in our custom He might capture us.

—Ephraim the Syrian, *Hymns of the Nativity*

Reality of the Incarnation

When you hear that "the Word was made flesh," do not be disturbed nor disheartened. . . . Why does he use the expression "was made"? To stop the mouths of heretics. For since there are some who are saying that the whole of the Incarnation was a fantasy and a show and an illusion he put down that "was made" to take away their blasphemy beforehand, intending to show thereby not a change of essence, perish the thought, but the assumption of true flesh.

—John Chrysostom, *Homilies on the Gospel of John*

If the incarnation was a phantasm, so too is salvation a phantasm.

—Cyril of Jerusalem, *Catechetical Lectures*

It would not have been fitting for One who accomplished a perfect work in others to allow anything imperfect in Himself.

If something was lacking in His humanity, He did not redeem the whole man; and if He did not redeem the whole man, He was a deceiver when He declared that He had come to save the whole man. But He did not deceive. . . . His humanity was perfect.

—Ambrose of Milan, *Letter to Sabinus*

He became man; He did not merely enter into a man.

—Athanasius, *Orations Against the Arians*

For human reason would take it to be far more difficult for God to become man than for a man to be reckoned a son of God.

—John Chrysostom, *Homilies on the Gospel of Matthew*

We maintain . . . that what has been laid aside in Christ is not the flesh of sin, but the sin of the flesh.

—Tertullian, *The Flesh of Christ*

For though all flesh is sinful, yet He had flesh without sin, and had in Himself the likeness of sinful flesh. . . .

—John Cassian, *The Seven Books*

N.B.

Glory to that Hidden One, Whose Son was made manifest!
Glory to that Living One, Whose Son was made to die!
Glory to that Great One, Whose Son descended and was small!
Glory to the Power Who did straiten His greatness by a form,
His unseen nature by a shape!

—Ephraim the Syrian, *Hymns on the Nativity*

Instruction

(See also: School of Christ)

Why are the unlearned ever so rash as to undertake the care of teaching, when the art of teaching is the art of all arts? Who does not know that the wounds of the mind are more obscure than the wounds of the body?

—Gregory the Great, *Pastoral Care*

She must not therefore learn as a child what afterwards she will have to unlearn.

—Jerome, *Letter to Laeta*

He must strive to live so as to moisten the dried-up hearts with the flowing waves of his instruction.

—Gregory the Great, *Pastoral Care*

N.B.

Let some holy volume be ever in your hand.

—Jerome, *Letter to Paulinus*

Intellect

(See also: Mind; Reason)

You are not much different from cattle, except that you have intelligence; so do not glory in anything else. Do you claim to be strong? You will be beaten by beasts. Do you claim speed? Flies are faster. Do you claim beauty? What great beauty there is in a peafowl's feathers! How are you better, then, than these? By the image of God. And where is God's image? In your mind, in your intellect!

—Augustine, *Homilies on John*

There are three things: to exist, to live, to understand; even a stone exists, and a beast lives, yet I do not think that a stone lives, or that a beast understands. But he who understands assuredly both exists and lives; wherefore I do not hesitate to judge that one more excellent in which all three are present.

—Augustine, *On Free Choice*

⇴ Caution

The poverty of human intelligence is often involved in lengthy discussions because questions require more words than answers. . . .

—Augustine, *Confessions*

The rude and simple brother must not suppose himself a saint just because he knows nothing; and he who is educated must not measure his saintliness merely by his fluency.

—Jerome, *Letter to Nepotian*

These three kinds of vision, therefore, namely, corporeal, spiritual, and intellectual, must be considered separately so that the reason may ascend from the lower to the higher. We have already proposed above an example by which all three kinds are illustrated in one sentence. For when we read: "Thou shalt love thy neighbor as thyself," the letters are seen corporeally, the neighbor is thought of spiritually, and love is beheld intellectually.

—Augustine, *Literal Commentary on Genesis*

Judgment

Hear the other side.

—Augustine, *De Duabus Animabus*

Day of Judgment

The Day of Judgment betokens an eternal measuring out either of happiness or of punishment.

—Hilary of Poitiers, *Commentaries on the Psalms*

You are fond of spectacles, except the greatest of all spectacles —that last eternal Day of Judgment.

—Tertullian, *De Spectaculis*

Certain and thorough

Thou threatenest me with fire which burneth for an hour, and after a little is extinguished, but art ignorant of the fire of the coming judgment and of eternal punishment, reserved for the ungodly. But why tarriest thou? Bring forth what thou wilt.

—Polycarp, to the proconsul who tried him

We are so far from practising promiscuous intercourse that we are not even allowed a lustful glance. What could justify any doubt as to the purity of the life led by those who are not allowed to use their eyes for any other purpose than that for which God created them, namely to look in the light for whom even a lustful glance is called adultery! For them the coming judgment applies even to thoughts.

—Athenagoras, *A Plea Regarding Christians*

Benefits of self-judgment

But when lust overcame him and took Bathsheba, the wife of Uriah, the Scripture said about him, "The thing which David did was wicked in the eyes of the Lord." And the prophet Nathan was sent to him to show him his sin. Thus he had to pass sentence upon himself and condemn himself so that he could obtain mercy and forgiveness from Christ.

—Irenaeus, *Against Heresies*

For He never makes a public display of our sins, except at any time He sees men insensible to them.

—John Chrysostom, *The Omnipotent Christ*

Blushing for shame you will be dragged before the public. That is good for you, for he who is not publicly exposed like this before men will be publicly exposed before God.

—Tertullian, *On Flight in Persecution*

Judgment of others

Know that in judging others you are passing sentence on yourself.

—Jerome, *Letter to Nepotian*

An arrow never lodges in a stone: often it recoils upon the shooter of it.

—Jerome, *Letter to Nepotian*

Justification

Indeed, what else could have covered over our sins except His righteousness? In whom was it possible for us, in view of our wickedness and impiety, to be justified, except in the Son of God alone? Oh, the sweet exchange! Oh, the unfathomable accomplishment! Oh, the unexpected benefits!—that the wickedness of the many should be hidden in the One who is just; and that the righteousness of the One should justify the wicked many!

—Letter to Diognetus

The Scriptures and the facts themselves oblige us to confess that Abraham received circumcision for a sign and not for justification.

—Justin, *Dialogue with Trypho the Jew*

He who made you without your consent does not justify you without your consent.

—Augustine, *Sermons*

Kingdom of God

God whom all creation serves always has a kingdom, and is never without a kingdom.

—Augustine, *The Lord's Prayer Explained*

The violent take it

"The Kingdom of heaven suffereth violence and the violent take it by force." . . . Who then are the violent? Surely they are those who show a splendid violence not to others, but to their own soul, who by a laudable force deprive it of all delights in the things present, and are declared by the Lord's mouth to be splendid plunderers, and by rapine of this kind, violently seize upon the Kingdom of heaven.

—John Cassian, *Conference of Abbot Abraham*

". . . and the violent take it by force." Such was the conduct of the robber, more courageous on the cross than in the place of ambush.

—Augustine, *Psalms*

". . . the publicans and the harlots go into the Kingdom of God before you." They go before because they do violence; they push their way by faith, and to faith a way is made nor can any resist, since they who are violent take it by force.

—Augustine, *Psalms*

God overrules

The emperor Julian found time during his Parthian campaign to vomit forth seven books against Christ and, as so often happens in poetic legends, only wounded himself with his own sword.

—Jerome

Knowledge

Know that it is the voice of scoffers that says: "If you are ignorant of the essence of God, you adore what you do not know." I know He is; but what His essesnce is, that I regard as beyond understanding. How, then, am I saved? Through faith. Faith suffices in itself to know that God is, not what He is.

—Basil the Great, *Letter to Amphilochius, Bishop of Iconium*

Let us learn upon earth that knowledge which will continue with us in heaven.

—Jerome, *Letter to Paulinus*

. . . nor is he far from knowledge, who begins to understand how ignorant he is.

—John Cassian, *The Second Conference of Abbot Isaac*

The man who joins action to knowledge is strong: by the first, he curbs covetousness and calms anger; by the second, he gives wings to his spirit and emigrates toward God. . . .

—Maximus, *The Centuries on Charity*

❧ Knowledge or faith . . . which first?

Which is first, knowledge or faith? We say that in general, in the case of the mathematical sciences, faith precedes knowledge. But if in our teaching, anyone says that knowledge comes before faith, I raise no objection, rather taking knowledge as referring to the knowledge that is within the limits of human comprehension.

—Basil the Great, *Letter to Amphilochius, Bishop of Iconium*

Law

There have been in the whole period of the duration of the world two conspicuous changes of men's lives . . . or . . . two earthquakes; the one from idols to the law, the other from the law to the Gospel.

—Gregory of Nazianzus, *On the Holy Spirit*

You must not have a monopoly of bending the law to suit your will instead of bending your will to suit the law.

—Jerome, *Letter to Oceanus*

Liberality

Marks

That liberality is real where a man hides what he does in silence, and secretly assists the needs of individuals, whom the mouth of the poor, and not his own lips, praises.

—Ambrose, *Rules for Christian Living*

Do good, and with a simple heart share the fruits of your labour which God gives to you with those who are poor, not wondering to whom you should give and to whom you should not give. Give all, for God wishes that you give to all from His gifts to you.

—Hermas, *The Shepherd*

It is no sign of a liberal spirit to extort from one what we give to another.

—Ambrose, *Rules for Christian Living*

Noble woman, who found something much greater to give to the emperor than she could receive from the emperor.

—Ambrose, *On the Death of Theodosius*

We . . . cannot refrain from turning the cheek when we are struck, nor from blessing when we are reviled. For, it is not enough to be just—justice consisting in returning blows—but we have to be generous.

—Athenagoras, *A Plea Regarding Christians*

The ultimate liberality

To whom then are you to leave your great riches? To Christ who cannot die.

—Jerome, *Letter to Furia*

We know of many among our number who have given themselves up freewilling to imprisonment so that they might bring freedom to others. Many have sold themselves into slavery to feed others with the money they received.

—Clement, *First Letter to the Corinthians*

Guidelines

Give your riches not to those who feed on pheasants but to those who have none but common bread to eat, such as stays hunger while it does not stimulate lust.

—Jerome, *Letter to Furia*

It is a serious fault if a believer is in want, and thou knowest it.

—Ambrose, *Rules for Christian Living*

And this saying is above all divinity—not to wait to be asked, but to inquire oneself who deserves to receive kindness.

—Clement of Alexandria, *Who Is the Rich Man That Shall Be Saved?*

These are, as it were, the deposits of piety. For they are not expended therefrom on feasts and drinking parties and in thankless houses of gluttony, but for the support and burial of the poor, for boys and girls without parents and destitute of means, for the aged quietly confined to their homes, for the shipwrecked; and if there are any in the mines or in the islands or in the prisons, if it be for the reason that they are worshippers of God, then they become the foster-sons of their confession.

—Tertullian, *Apology*

Do not . . . by an error of judgment give the property of the poor to those who are not poor; lest, as a wise man has told us, charity prove the death of charity.

—Jerome, *Letter to Paulinus*

What if my gift is misused?

Give to all, for God wishes His gifts to be shared amongst all. They who receive, will render an account to God why and for what they have received. For the afflicted who receive will not be condemned, but they who receive on false pretences will suffer punishment. He, then, who gives is guiltless. For as he received from the Lord, so has he accomplished his service in simplicity, not hesitating as to whom he should give and to whom he should not give.

—Hermas, *The Shepherd*

Besides food and clothing and things manifestly necessary give no man anything.

—Jerome, *Letter to Paulinus*

Thus you will give to every one that asketh you, although you will not always give what he asks.

—Augustine, *Our Lord's Sermon on the Mount*

N.B.

Whosoever does a kindness lends at interest.

—Augustine, *Our Lord's Sermon on the Mount*

Beware, lest you be like the men of earth, who, when they awaken in another world, awake with empty hands because they placed nothing in Christ's hands, which were streched out to them in the hands of His poor and needy.

—Augustine

Liberty

To yield and give way to our passions is the lowest slavery, even as to rule over them is the only liberty.

—Justin, quoted by Antonius Melissa

The Apostle taught me, however, that beyond freedom itself there is a freedom to serve.

—Ambrose of Milan, *Letter to Simplician*

The slave might be superior in character to his master and be really more free than he.

—Ambrose of Milan

For he is freely in bondage who does with pleasure the will of his master.

—Augustine, *Enchiridion*

"Liberty in Christ" has done no injury to innocence.

—Tertullian, *On Modesty*

He who is the servant of sin is free to sin. And hence he will not be free to do right, until, being freed from sin, he shall begin to be the servant of righteousness. And this is true liberty. . . .

—Augustine, *Enchiridion*

We shall be made truly free, then, when God fashions us, that is, forms and creates us anew, not as men—for He has done that already—but as good men, which His grace is now doing.

—Augustine, *Enchiridion*

Therefore the good man, although he is a slave, is free; but the bad man, even if he reigns, is a slave, and that not of one man, but, what is far more grievous, of as many masters as he has vices.

—Augustine, *The City of God*

Life

If that man first formed out of the earth ushered in universal death, shall not He that formed him out of the earth bring in eternal life, since He Himself is life?

—Cyril of Jerusalem, *Catechetical Lectures*

A general cannot give what he does not possess; he cannot prolong life, although he can reward service. But the soldier of God is neither abandoned in trouble nor destroyed by death.

—Minucius Felix, *Octavius*

Light

". . . which lighteneth every man . . ."

The one and only God was known by the Greeks in a Gentile

way, by the Jews Judaically, and in a new and spiritual way by us.

—Clement of Alexandria, *The Stromata*

Perchance, too, philosophy was given to the Greeks directly and primarily, till the Lord should call the Greeks. For this was a schoolmaster to bring "the Hellenic mind," as the law, the Hebrews, "to Christ."

—Clement of Alexandria, *The Stromata*

And so . . . Plato, when he says, "The blame is his who chooses, and God is blameless," took this from the prophet Moses and uttered it. For Moses is more ancient than all the Greek writers. And whatever both philosophers and poets have said concerning the immortality of the soul, or punishments after death, or contemplation of things heavenly, or doctrines of the like kind, they have received such suggestions from the prophets as have enabled them to understand and interpret these things. And hence there seem to be seeds of truth among all men; but they are charged with not accurately understanding (the truth) when they assert contradictories.

—Justin, *The First Apology*

Noble philosophers too have sought these things, and have recognized the Artisan by the art.

—Augustine, *Sermons*

The unenlightened?

If He "enlightens every many who comes into the world," how is it that there are some who remain unenlightened? . . . If there are some who choose to close the eyes of their mind and do not want to receive the rays of that light, their darkness comes not from the nature of the light, but from their own wickedness in voluntarily depriving themselves of that gift.

—John Chrysostom, *Homilies on the Gospel of John*

Love

Love . . . is so much the gift of God that it is called God.

—Augustine, *Letter to Paulinus of Nova*

I do not exhort you to have faith, but love. For you cannot have love without faith. . . . How can he love God, who does not believe in God?

—Augustine, *Sermons*

My weight is my love.

—Augustine, *Confessions*

And the preeminent gift of love, which is more precious than knowledge, more glorious than prophecy, and more honoured than all the other charismatic gifts.

—Irenaeus, *Against Heresies*

He gave you faith, hope and love: this you can offer, this you can sacrifice. But plainly, everything else can be taken from you against your will by an enemy; but this cannot be taken from you unless you are willing.

—Augustine, *Psalms*

Love, of all science the most sacred and most sovereign.

—Clement of Alexandria, *The Stromata*

Embrace the love of God, and by love embrace God.

—Augustine, *On the Trinity*

When the thing hoped for actually comes, all the other faculties are idled and love alone remains active, finding nothing to succeed itself.

—Gregory of Nyssa, *Dialogue on the Soul and Resurrection*

He (God) hates nothing in man except sin.

—Augustine, *Questions for Simplicianus*

Late have I loved Thee, O Beauty so ancient and so new, late have I loved Thee! And behold, Thou wert within and I was without. I was looking for Thee out there, and I threw myself, deformed as I was, upon those well-formed things which Thou hast made. Thou wert with me, yet I was not with Thee. These things held me far from Thee, things which would not have existed had they not been in Thee. Thou didst call and cry out and burst in upon my deafness; Thou didst shine forth and glow and drive away my blindness; Thou didst send forth Thy fragrance, and I drew in my breath and now I pant for Thee; I have tasted, and now I hunger and thirst; Thou didst touch me, and I was inflamed with desire for Thy peace.

—Augustine, *Confessions*

Love one another

When the blessed Evangelist John, the apostle, had lived in Ephesus into his extreme old age and could hardly be carried to the meetings of the Church by the disciples anymore, and when in speaking he could no longer put together many words, he would not say anthing else in the different meetings but this: "Little children, love one another!" When at last the disciple and brothers present got tired of hearing the same thing again and again, they said, "Master, why do you keep saying the same thing?" John replied with a saying worthy of him: "Because it is the Lord's command, and it is enough if it is really done."

—Jerome, *Commentary on Galatians*

We love one another, since we do not know how to hate.

—Minucius Felix, *Octavius*

There is no nation of so barbarous a behavior and so ignorant of civility, that it has not, under the influence of His love, softened its harshness, . . . and passed over into peaceful dispositions.

—Arnobius of Sicca, *Against the Pagans*

Higher ground—love your enemies

The prophet Isaiah tells us that we should not, as some think, love only your own: Say to those that hate and curse you, "You are our brothers!" And the Gospel says, "Love your enemies!"

—Theophilus of Antioch

Love those who hate you, and you will not have an enemy.

—Didache

If thou lovest the good disciples only, thou hast no grace; rather subdue those that are evil by gentleness.

—Ignatius, *Epistle to Polycarp*

If you love the good disciples it does not bring you any credit; rather restore the corrupted ones by kindness. Not every wound is healed with the same plaster.

—Ignatius, *Letter to Polycarp*

In no way can a vicious enemy hurt you as much as you hurt yourself by not loving that enemy.

—Augustine, *The Lord's Prayer Explained*

Loving the sinner and not the sin

Loving one's enemies does not mean loving wickedness, or impiety, or adultery, or theft, but the thief, the impious, the adulterer, not as far as he sins, and in respect of the actions by which he stains the name of the man, but as he is a man, and the work of God.

—Clement of Alexandria, *The Stromata*

⇔ Look deeper

We can find a man made savage by love and another made gentle by iniquity. A father beats a boy, and a seducer of boys caresses. If you but name the two actions, who would not choose the caresses and decline the blows? But if you take note of persons whose actions they are, it is love that beats the boy and iniquity that caresses him.

—Augustine, *Homilies on the Epistle of John*

Someone who does not love believes in vain even if what he believes is true.

—Augustine, *Enchiridion of Faith, Hope, and Love*

⇔ Motive par excellence

O my God, for love of Thy love I do it.

—Augustine, *Confessions*

I define love as a movement of the mind directed to the enjoyment of God for his own sake, and self and neighbor for the sake of God.

—Augustine, *On Christian Doctrine*

No sinner is to be loved as a sinner; and every man is to be loved as a man for God's sake; but God is to be loved for His own sake.

—Augustine, *On Christian Doctrine*

⇔ N.B.

A short precept, therefore, is given you: Love, and do what you will.

—Augustine, *Homilies on the Epistle of John*

Lust

(See also: Sex)

Attempts at definition

Lust . . . is a movement of the mind directed to the enjoyment of self and neighbor and whosesoever's body, not for the sake of God.

—Augustine, *Christian Instruction*

The first man, when he was in Paradise, played in childlike abandon, because he was a child of God; but when he gave himself over to pleasure . . . he was seduced by lust, and in disobedience the child became a man.

—Clement of Alexandria, *Exhortation to the Greeks*

It is one thing, they say, to sin with the body, and another to sin in the body.

—Jerome, *Letter to Amandus*

It is unlawful even to desire that which it is unlawful to do.

—Sulpitius Severus, *Letter to Claudia*

Recipes for victory

A soul which is contained by a concupiscent body, and which appeases with the medicaments of temperance the disorders arising from the heat of lusts, carries off the palm for healing, over one to whose lot it has fallen to govern aright a body which is free from lust.

—Methodius of Olympus, *The Banquet of the Ten Virgins*

It is for us Christians to restrain the desire for sensual indulgence by an intenser love for Christ.

—Jerome, *Letter to Salvian*

By a cold chastity she seeks to put out the flame of lust and to quench the hot desire of youth.

—Jerome, *Letter to Laeta*

Oppose the flames of eternal punishment to the fire of concupiscence.

—Isidore of Seville, *A Dialogue Between the Erring Soul and Reason*

Let every holy woman guard herself from desiring sinfully to please man by cherishing a fear of displeasing God.

—Augustine, *Letter to the Nuns*

The eyes especially are to be sparingly used, since it is better to slip with the feet than with the eyes.

—Clement of Alexandria, *The Instructor*

Its power

It is exceedingly disgraceful that lust should subdue him whom man finds invincible.

—Augustine, *To Publicola*

All such sins as theft, manslaughter, pillage, perjury, and the like can be repented of after they have been committed; and however much interest may tempt him, conscience always smites the offender. It is only lust and sensual pleasure that in the very hour of penitence undergo once more the temptations of the past, the itch of the flesh, and the allurements of sin; so that the very thought which we bestow on the correction of such transgressions becomes in itself a new source of sin.

—Jerome, *Letter to Amandus*

When the body is heated with drink it soon boils over with lust.

—Jerome, *Letter to Oceanus*

It is because of concupiscence that even in the righteous and legitimate marriage of the children of God, not children of God but children of the world are begotten. . . .

—Augustine, *Marriage and Concupiscence*

Under sentence

In amplifying His law God makes no distinction of penalty between lust and fornication.

—Tertullian, *On Female Dress*

Every one who twists the oracles of the Lord to his own lusts, and denies the resurrection and the judgment to come, he is the first-born of Satan.

—Polycarp

Man

What is man?

. . . a soul using a body.

—Augustine, *On the Moral Behavior of the Catholic Church*

King of all upon the earth, but subject to the King above.

—Gregory of Nazianzus, *On the Theophany*

Man, who among the things that exist is reckoned as nothing, as ashes, as grass, as vanity, is made the familiar of such and so great a Majesty as can neither be seen, nor heard, nor reckoned. Man is received and accounted as son by the God of the universe.

—Gregory of Nyssa, *The Beatitudes*

Man is a good thing spoiled.

—Augustine

For he who in the light of day denies his manhood, will prove himself manifestly a woman by night.

—Clement of Alexandria, *The Instructor*

Man consists of these three elements: spirit, soul, and body—

which sometimes are reckoned as two, for often soul is included in the destination of spirit—our chief element is the spirit.

—Augustine, *Faith and the Creed*

His creation

Do you see how all things were created by a word? But let us see what it says afterwards about the creation of man: "And God shaped man." See how, by means of a condescension of terms employed for the sake of our weakness, it teaches at the same time both the manner of creation and its diversity or variety, so that, speaking in human terms, it indicates that man was shaped by the very hands of God.

—John Chrysostom, *Homilies on Genesis*

Nor is it a matter of difference that the woman was not formed of the same clay from which Adam was made, but was made from the rib of Adam himself, so that we might know that the flesh of man and woman is of but one nature, and that there is but one source of the human race. . . . He snatched away the possibility of numerous and desperate natures.

—Ambrose of Milan, *Paradise*

The sun was formed by a mere command, but man by God's hands.

—Cyril of Jerusalem, *Lecture XII*

Why was he created?

In the beginning God formed Adam, not as if needing him, but that He might have someone on whom to bestow His benefits.

—Irenaeus, *Against Heresies*

(God) created man, not that He might Himself profit in any way by man's service, but because He is good. He made him for the sharing of His own happiness. . . .

—Hilary of Poitiers, *Commentaries on the Psalms*

Paths to perfection

If one knows himself, he will know God; and knowing God, he will be made like God.

—Clement of Alexandria, *The Instructor*

The more then a man hastes to the end, the more truly venerable is he, having God alone as his senior.

—Clement of Alexandria, *The Instructor*

The majesty of God cannot be propitiated by that which defiles the dignity of man.

—Augustine, *The City of God*

The man, who would be beautiful, must adorn that which is the most beautiful thing in man, his mind.

—Clement of Alexandria, *The Instructor*

It was the ground that God cursed, not Adam. And He cursed the serpent; and the fire was prepared originally for the devil and his angels, not for man.

—Irenaeus

N.B.

And if every one ought not to trust in man, surely not himself; because he is a man.

—Augustine, *On the Psalms*

Marriage

. . . the seminary of the human race.

—Tertullian, *To his wife*

Monogamy

We (Christians) have all things in common, except our wives.

—Tertullian

Second best?

"It is better to marry than to burn." . . . But if marriage is only a degree better than the evil to which it is preferred, it cannot be of that unblemished perfection and blessedness.

—Jerome, *Letter to Pammachius*

I have dealt more gently with marriage than most Latin and Greek writers; who, by referring the hundredfold yield to martyrs, the sixtyfold to virgins, and the thirtyfold to widows, show that in their opinion married persons are excluded from the good ground and from the seed of the great Father.

—Jerome, *Letter to Pammachius*

For the Church does not condemn marriage, but only subordinates it. It does not reject it altogether, but regulates it.

—Jerome, *Letter to Pammachius*

His (Paul) words are these: "I will therefore that the younger women marry, bear children, guide the house, give none occasion to the adversary to speak reproachfully." But he immediately adds as a reason for this concession: "for some are already turned aside after Satan." Thus we see that he is offering not a crown to those who stand but a helping hand to those who are down. What must a second marriage be if it is to be looked on merely as an alternative to the brothel! "For some," he writes, "are already turned aside after Satan." The upshot of the whole matter is that, if a young widow cannot or will not contain herself, she had better take a husband to her bed than the devil.

—Jerome, *Letter to Salvina*

Only consider for a moment that it was the virgins who merited to witness the Lord's resurrection even ahead of the apostles.

—Ambrose of Milan, *Virginity*

The difference between marriage and virginity is as great as that between not doing evil and doing good.

—Jerome, *Letter to Pammachius*

We learn from the apostle, who *permits* marrying indeed, but *prefers* abstinence. . . .

—Tertullian, *To his wife*

Wives, be ye subject to your husbands in the fear of God; and ye virgins, to Christ in purity, not counting marriage an abomination, but desiring that which is better not for the reproach of wedlock, but for the sake of meditating on the law.

—Ignatius, *Epistle to the Philadelphians*

Beg to differ!

I see that God regards not whether one is virgin or married, whether one is in a monastery or the world: He considers only the dispostion of the heart, and gives the Spirit to all who desire to serve Him, whatever their condition may be.

—Macarius

Marital intercourse makes something good out of an evil appetite.

—Augustine, *The Advantage of Marriage*

Second marriage

And those who are once married—let them not hold in contempt those who have accommodated themselves to a second marriage. Continence is a good and wonderful thing; but still, it is permissable to enter upon a second marriage, lest the weak might fall into fornication.

—Cyril of Jerusalem, *Catechetical Lectures*

What then? Do we condemn second marriage? Not at all; but we praise first marriages. Do we expel bigamists from the Church? Far from it; but we urge the once-married to continence.

—Jerome, *Letter to Pammachius*

What we suggest by way of counsel we do not command as a precept. We do not so much bind the widow as encourage her. We do not prohibit second marriages, but neither do we recommend them. Consideration of weakness is one thing, the grace of chastity another.

—Ambrose of Milan, *The Widows*

N.B.

Wedlock is like a plank offered to a shipwrecked man and by its means you may remedy what previously you have done amiss.

—Jerome, *Letter to a mother and daughter living in Gaul*

Martyrdom

The whole earth has been crimsoned by the blood of Martyrs; heaven is flowery with the crowns of Martyrs, the churches are adorned with the memorials of Martyrs, seasons distinguished by the birthdays of Martyrs. . . .

—Augustine, *On Psalm 119*

Definition

An associate of Christ's passion in Christ's name.

—Letter to Cyprian from certain presbyters, etc.

⇼ Voice of the martyrs

Fire and the sword, beasts of prey, irons to rend the flesh, are an indulgence rather than a terror to a Christian.

—Gregory of Nazianzus, *Dialogue Between Basil and Modestus*

You may kill us, but you can never hurt us.

—Justin Martyr

Eighty-six years I have served Him, and He has never done me wrong. How, then, should I be able to blaspheme my King who has saved me?

—Polycarp's answer to the Proconsul in Smyrna

Accustom your limbs rather to fetters than to bracelets of gold; on the neck of yours now encircled with chains of pearls and emeralds, leave a spot where the sword of the lictor can fall. . . . The robes which the angels are bringing you, remember, are the robes of martyrdom.

—Tertullian

May I have joy of the beasts that have been prepared for me; and I pray that I may find them prompt; nay I will entice them that they may devour me promptly, not as they have done to some. . . .

—Ignatius, *Letter to the Romans*

The refusal of martyrdom is denial.

—Tertullian, *De Fuga in Persecutione*

I am the wheat of God, and let me be ground by the teeth of the wild beasts, so that I may be found the pure bread of Christ.

—Ignatius, *Letter to the Romans*

He runs no risk of confiscation who has nothing to lose. . . .

Nor does he care for exile who is not circumscribed by place. . . . Nor can tortures harm a frame so frail as to break under the first blow. You could but strike once, and death would be gain. It would but send me the sooner to Him for whom I live and labour.

—Gregory of Nazianzus, *Dialogue Between Basil and Modestus*

It is better for me to be a martyr than a monarch.

—Ignatius

More than conquerors

I am assured that while I live I shall be the victor in my contest with you, and if you cause me to be put to death I shall be still more a conqueror.

—Felicitas before her execution

In the hour of their torture the martyrs of Christ were absent from the flesh, or rather that the Lord was present. . . . The fire of their inhuman torturers was cold to them, for their eyes were set on escape from the eternal fire.

—Euarestus, writing on behalf of the church in Smyrna

How is it, then, that the region of paradise which was revealed to John in the spirit, and which was beneath the altar, displays no souls therein except those of the martyrs? . . . The only key to paradise is your blood . . . every soul is detained in Hades until the day of the Lord.

—Tertullian, *The Soul*

The examination by torture waxing severer, continued for a long time to this result, not to overthrow the steadfast faith, but to send the men of God more quickly to the Lord.

—Cyprian, *Epistles*

Martyrdom is bringing forth fruit a hundredfold; voluntary celibacy sixtyfold.

—Cyprian, *Epistles*

The priest of God holding fast the Gospel and keeping Christ's precepts may be slain; he cannot be conquered.

—Cyprian, *Epistles*

Blood was flowing which might quench the blaze of persecution, which might subdue the flames of Gehenna with its glorious gore.

—Cyprian, *Epistles*

It is not martyrs that make the Gospel, but . . . martyrs are made by the Gospel.

—Cyprian, *Epistles*

By this very fact they are invincible, that they do not fear death.

—Cyprian, *Epistles*

Welcome Sister Death

If I suffer, it will be because you favoured me. If I am rejected, it will be because you hated me.

—Ignatius, *Letter to the Romans*

May nothing seen or unseen begrudge me making my way to Jesus Christ. Come fire, cross, battling with wild beasts, wrenching of bones, mangling of limbs, crushing of my whole body, cruel tortures of the devil—only let me get to Jesus Christ!

—Ignatius, *Letter to the Romans*

We conquer in dying.

—Tertullian

Two kinds of martyrs

There be . . . two kinds of martyrdoms, the one secret, the other open: for if a man hath a burning zeal in his mind to suffer death for Christ, although he endureth not any external persecution, yet hath he in secret the merit of martyrdom. For that one may be a martyr without suffering death openly, our Lord doth teach us in the Gospel.

—Gregory the Great, *Dialogues Concerning Martyrdom*

It is the cause, not the punishment, that makes martyrs.

—Augustine, *Psalms*

The injustice of it all

We should not be hated and punished because we are called Christians, for what has a name to do with our being criminals?

—Athenagoras, *A Plea Regarding Christians*

N.B.

Our altars are not set up to any one of the martyrs, although in their memory, but to God Himself, the God of those martyrs.

—Augustine, *Against Faustus*

Mary

Great is the mystery

The Babe that I carry carries me, saith Mary. . . .

—Ephraim the Syrian, *Hymns on the Nativity*

Mary was a virgin, in so far as a husband is concerned; and not a virgin, in so far as child-bearing is concerned.

—Tertullian, *The Flesh of Christ*

She became a mother at a leap, as it were, before she became a wife.

—Tertullian, *The Flesh of Christ*

She is at once both Virgin and Mother: as a Virgin, undefiled; as a Mother, full of love.

—Clement of Alexandria, *The Instructor of Children*

Eve had believed the serpent; Mary believed Gabriel.

—Tertullian, *The Flesh of Christ*

In accord with the realities of both natures, the same Virgin would be both handmaid of the Lord and His Mother also. . . .

—Gregory the Great, *Moral Teachings from Job*

Who loves you is amazed; and who would understand is silent and confused, because he cannot probe the Mother who gave birth in her virginity. If it is too great to be clarified with words the disputants ought not on that account cross swords with your Son.

—Ephraim the Syrian, *Songs of Praise*

Was not the Son of God existent before the daughter of man? . . . I do not merely say that Mary gave birth to one who had existed before her, not only, I say, one who had existed before her, but one who was the author of her being. . . .

—John Cassian, *The Seven Books*

The flesh of sin

For the flesh of Mary, which had been conceived in iniquities in the usual manner, was the flesh of sin which begot the Son of God in the likeness of the flesh of sin. . . . But when the likeness of the flesh of sin is in the Son of God, or rather, when the Son of God is said to be in the likeness of the flesh of sin, it does not mean that the Only-begotten God drew any stain of sin from the mortal flesh of the Virgin, but that He accepted the full reality of our nature.

—Fulgence of Ruspe, *Letters*

Mother of God?

Surely she must be the mother of God if our Lord Jesus Christ is God, and she gave birth to Him! Our Lord's disciples may not have used those exact words, but they delivered to us the belief those words enshrine.

—Cyril of Alexandria

When, therefore, they ask, "Is Mary Mother of Man or Mother of God?" We answer, "Both!" The one by the very nature of what was done, and the other by relation. Mother of Man, because it was a Man who was in the womb of Mary and who came forth from there; and Mother of God, because God was in the Man who was born. . . .

—Theodore of Mopsuestia, *The Incarnation*

Mary the Mother of our Lord Jesus Christ ought not to be called Theotocos, i.e., Mother of God, but Christotocos, i.e., only the Mother of Christ, not of God. For no one . . . brings forth what is anterior in time.

—Nestorius, quoted by John Cassian

N.B.

He . . . has on earth only a Mother, while we have in heaven only a Father.

—Athanasius, *Incarnation of the Word of God*

Meditation

. . . chewing the cud of this heavenly food.

—John Cassian, *The First Conference of Abbot Chaeremon*

Seek and find, and realize that the truth does not lie openly on the surface.

—Clement, *Homily 111*

Balance

No man has a right to lead such a life of contemplation as to forget in his own ease the service due to his neighbour; nor has any man a right to be so immersed in active life as to neglect the contemplation of God.

—Augustine

Mercy

We know that God's mercy is gratuitously given to those to whom it is given at all.

—Augustine, *Letter to Vitalis, layman of Carthage*

Divine mercy is such that it aids those who are willing.

—Hilary of Poitiers, *Commentaries on the Psalms*

One hope, one trust, one firm promise: Thy mercy!

—Augustine, *Confessions*

Let no one be less good because God is more so, by repeating his sins as often as he is forgiven. Otherwise be sure he will find an end of *escaping* when he shall not find one of *sinning*.

—Tertullian, *On Repentance*

That thou are righteous then, impute it wholly to His mercy; but that thou art a sinner, ascribe it to thine own iniquity.

—Augustine, *Sermons on New Testament Lessons*

N.B.

For here is great misery, proud man! But there is greater mercy, a humble God!

—Augustine, *On the Catechising of the Uninstructed*

In the family of the just man who lives by faith . . . even those who rule serve those whom they seem to command; for they rule not from a love of power, but from a sense of the duty they owe to others—not because they are proud of authority, but because they love mercy.

—Augustine, *City of God*

Mind

(See also: Intellect)

The man, who would be beautiful, must adorn that which is the most beautiful thing in man, his mind.

—Clement of Alexandria, *On the True Beauty*

Small minds can never handle great themes.

—Jerome, *Letter 60*

In your soul is the image of God; the human mind contains that image. It received it and by stooping to sin defiled it.

—Augustine, *On Psalms*

The Ministry

Clergy

It is on account of the Greek word *kleros,* which means in English "lot" or "inheritance," that the clergy are so called, either because they are of the lot of the Lord or because the Lord is Himself their lot or portion. And he that is the Lord's portion or who has the Lord for his portion must so conduct himself that he both possesses the Lord and is possessed by the Lord.

—Jerome, *Letter to Nepotian*

Having the keys of the Kingdom of Heaven, they judge men to some extent before the Day of Judgment, and guard the chastity of the bride of Christ.

—Jerome, *Letter to Heliodorus*

To be a bishop is much, to deserve to be one is more.

—Jerome, *Letter to Pammachius*

"If a man desire the office of a bishop, he desireth a good work." Work, you see, not rank.

—Jerome, *Letter to Oceanus*

Holiness plus . . .

Knowledge of the Scriptures is also necessary for him, because if a bishop is merely a holy man he benefits only himself, but if he is learned in doctrine and in speech, he can instruct others. . . .

—Isidore of Seville, *The Perfection of the Clergy*

A presbyter's word ought to be seasoned by his reading of Scripture.

—Jerome, *Letter to Nepotian*

A Christian bishop then must be such that they who cavil at his religion may not venture to cavil at his life.

—Jerome, *Letter to Oceanus*

Perseverance

It had been better not to have begun what is good than to return back from it when begun.

—Gregory the Great, *To the Brethren Going to England*

More are the tempests which assail the soul of a bishop, than those storms which agitate the ocean. . . .

—John Chrysostom, *On the Priesthood*

Balance

He must show such humility and authority that he neither allows the vices of his subjects to increase because of excessive meekness nor through immoderate zeal exercises power with severity, but acts the more cautiously toward his subjects in proportion as he expects to be judged the more severely by Christ.

—Isidore of Seville, *The Perfection of the Clergy*

The pastors are to be fervidly zealous about the inner wants of their subjects, without neglecting the care of their outer wants.

—Gregory the Great, *Pastoral Care*

Motive

When teaching in church seek to call forth not plaudits but groans. Let the tears of your hearers be your glory.

—Jerome, *Letter to Nepotian*

There is nothing so easy as by sheer volubility to deceive a common crowd or an uneducated congregation: such most admire what they fail to understand.

—Jerome, *Letter to Nepotian*

Nor is that pastor serviceable or wise who so mingles the diseased and affected sheep with his flock as to contaminate the whole flock with the infection of the clinging evil.

—Cyprian, *Epistles*

For the king rules over unwilling subjects, the bishop over willing ones. The king compels submission by terror; the bishop exercises lordship by becoming a servant.

—Jerome, *Letter to Heliodorus*

Clergy and laity

Vain shall we be if we consider that what is not lawful for priests is lawful for the laity. Are not we of the laity also priests?

—Tertullian, *An Exhortation to Chastity*

Unworthy clergy

The people, in obedience to the precepts of the Lord and in the fear of God, ought to separate themselves from a sinful prelate, nor ought they associate themselves with the sacrifices of a sacrilegious priest, especially in as much as they have the power both of electing worthy priests and of refusing the unworthy.

—Cyprian, *To Certain Clergy and Laity of Spain*

That man shows himself to be thoroughly unworthy of this office, who fears not to buy the gift of God with money, and presumes to try to get by payment what he deserves not to have through grace.

—Gregory the Great, *To Childebert, King of the Franks*

Let him not desire to intercede for the sins of others who is disgraced with his own.

—Gregory the Great, *Pastoral Care*

Not all bishops are bishops indeed. You consider Peter; mark Judas as well. You notice Stephen; look also on Nicolas, sentenced in the Apocalypse by the Lord's own lips. . . . For it is not ecclesiastical rank that makes a man a Christian.

—Jerome, *Letter to Heliodorus*

A clergyman who engages in business, and who rises from poverty to wealth, and from obscurity to a high position, avoid as you would the plague.

—Jerome, *Letter to Nepotian*

Harm done to the flock brings discredit on the shepherd.

—Jerome, *Letter to Furia*

Miracles

A portent . . . does not happen contrary to nature, but contrary to what we know about nature.

—Augustine, *The City of God*

It is agreed on that Christ performed all those miracles which He wrought without any aid from external things, without the observance of any ceremonial, without any definite mode of procedure, *but solely* by the inherent might of His authority.

—Arnobius, *Against the Heathen*

The governing of the whole world is a greater miracle than the feeding of five thousand men with five loaves of bread.

—Augustine, *Homilies on John*

In truth it is a greater miracle to root out from one's own flesh the incentives to wantonness than to cast out unclean spirits from the bodies of others.

—John Cassian, *The Second Conference of Abbot Nesteros*

But if they do not believe that these miracles were wrought by the apostles of Christ so that they might be believed when they preached the Resurrection and Ascension of Christ, this one grand miracle is enough for us, that the whole world has believed without any miracles.

—Augustine, *The City of God*

Let us ask the miracles themselves what they tell us of Christ; for if they be understood, they have a tongue of their own. For because Christ Himself is the Word of God, even the deed of the Word is word for us.

—Augustine, *Homilies on John*

N

Nativity

(See also: Incarnation; Virgin Birth)

He who is not carnal is Incarnate; the Son of God becomes the Son of Man.

—Gregory of Nazianzus, *On the Theophany*

Thy babe is aged, O Virgin, —and Ancient of Days and exalted above all; and Adam beside Him is very babe. . . .

—Ephraim the Syrian, *Hymns for the Feast of the Epiphany*

He that was without Mother becomes without Father.

—Gregory of Nazianzus, *On the Theophany*

On the one hand Being, and eternally Being, of the Eternal Being, above cause and word, for there was no word before the Word; and on the other hand for our sakes also Becoming, that He Who gives us our being might also give us our Well-being.

—Gregory of Nazianzus, *On the Theophany*

N.B.

The Magi exalted from afar; the Scribes murmured near at hand . . . the Scribes showed their doctrine, the Magi showed their offerings. It is a marvel that to Him, the Babe, they of His own house hasted with their swords, and they that were strangers with their offerings.

—Ephraim the Syrian, *Hymns on the Nativity*

Once, in Paradise, you (man) were so eloquent that you gave a name to every living being; but your Creator, because of you, lay speechless, and did not even call his mother by name. You, finding yourself in a boundless estate of fruitful groves, destroyed yourself by having no regard for obedience; He, obedient, came as a mortal man to a poor, tiny lodging that by dying He might seek the return of him who had died. You, though you were only man, wished to be God; and you were lost. He, though He was God, wished to be man that He might find what had been lost. Human pride pressed you down so that divine humility alone could lift you up

—Augustine, *Sermon on Christmas*

Oaths

"Swear not at all"; words which were in my opinion spoken, not because it is a sin to swear a true oath, but because it is a heinous sin to forswear oneself.

—Augustine, *To Publicola*

Can a broken oath be justified?

The blessed David determined and confirmed it by an oath, saying: "May God do so and add more to the foes of David if I leave of all that belong unto Nabal until the morning a single male." And presently when Abigail his wife interceded and intreated for him, he gave up his threats, lightened the sentence, and preferred to be regarded as a breaker of his word rather than to keep his pledged oath by cruelly executing it. . . .

—John Cassian, *Second Conference of Abbot Joseph*

We ought not obstinately to stick to our determination, but that we should with gentle pity soften down the threats which necessity called forth.

—John Cassian, *Second Conference of Abbot Joseph*

Obedience

Only when I am commanded to deny Him, will I not obey.

—Tatian, *Address to the Greeks*

For he who makes it his purpose to please men cannot please God, since the multitude choose not what is profitable, but what is pleasant.

—Clement of Alexandria, *The Stromata*

It is our duty, not to lead religion whither we would, but rather to follow religion whither it leads.

—Vincent of Lerins, *A Commonitory*

"Honor thy father," the commandment says, but only if he does not separate you from your true Father.

—Jerome, *Letter to Furia*

It is not the fact that it is good which binds us to obey, but the fact that God has enjoined it.

—Tertullian, *On Repentance*

The Savior asks neither what is impossible, nor what is impracticable, nor what is contrary to the will of the Father.

—Dionysius the Great, *Exegetical Fragments*

Give what Thou commandest, and command what Thou wilt.

—Augustine, *Confessions*

N.B.

Why debate? God commands.

—Tertullian

Old Age

Moses . . . in choosing the seventy elders is told to take those whom he knows to be elders indeed, and to select them not for their years but for their discretion.

—Jerome, *Letter to Paulinus*

How many there are nowadays who have lived so long that they bear corpses rather than bodies. . . .

—Jerome, *Letter to Paulinus*

N.B.

A newly kindled heat is more effective than a long continued lukewarmness.

—Jerome, *Letter to Paulinus*

Ordination

Even here in the Church the gradations of bishops, presbyters, and deacons happen to be imitations, in my opinion, of the angelic glory and of that arrangement which, the Scriptures say, awaits those who have followed in the footsteps of the Apostles.

—Clement of Alexandria, *The Stromata*

God commanded a priest to be appointed before all the congregation; that is, He instructs and shows us that the ordination of priests ought only to be solemnized with the knowledge of the people standing by.

—Cyprian

When a serving brother is ordained he receives the laying on of hands by the overseer. On a confessor who has been imprisoned hands shall not be laid for the service of deacon or that of elder, for he already has this honour by virtue of his confession.

—Hippolytus, *The Apostolic Tradition*

Pardon

(See also: Forgiveness)

Let no one cheat himself, let no one deceive himself: The Lord alone can have mercy. He alone can bestow pardon for sins which have been committed against Himself. . . .

—Cyprian, *On the Unity of the Church*

Sin is effaced neither by tears nor by penitence; neither angel nor archangel can remove its stain; God and God only, can take away sin.

—Ambrose of Milan

The wonderful thing is not simply that God forgives our sins, but He does this without revealing them or making them manifest and evident.

—John Chyrsostom, *Baptismal Catecheses*

Forgiveness of sins is a grace which is given with no antecedent merit.

—Augustine, *Letter to Sixtus*

He who despairs of pardon for his sin, damns himself by despair rather than by the crime he has committed. . . .

—Isidore of Seville, *A Dialogue Between the Erring Soul and Reason*

. . . for he loveth most, to whom most is forgiven.

—Augustine, *Psalms*

If there be repentance, pardon will on that account be granted for every sin, whether committed in flesh or in spirit, whether in deed or in desire, by the same God who otherwise determines their punishment in the judgment.

—Tertullian, *Repentance*

So is the cessation from sin the root of pardon, that pardon may be the fruit of repentance.

—Tertullian, *On Modesty*

N.B.

Vain is the penance stained by subsequent sin; a reopened wound heals more slowly; you will scarcely merit pardon, alternately weeping and sinning.

—Isidore of Seville, *A Dialogue Between the Erring Soul and Reason*

Patience

It was not divine power but divine patience that hardened Pharaoh.

—Caesar of Arles, *Sermons*

Peace

Peace is a good so great, that even in this earthly and mortal life there is no word we hear with such pleasure, nothing we desire with such zest or find to be more thoroughly gratifying.

—Augustine, *City of God*

It is not in war, but in peace, that we are trained.

—Clement of Alexandria, *The Paedagogus*

We ourselves were well conversant with war, murder, and everything evil, but all of us throughout the whole wide earth have traded in our weapons of war.

—Justin, *Dialogue with Trypho*

I pray you, O light of the dying, that mother may rest well. Aschandius, father, beloved of my soul, with my sweet mother and brothers in the peace of the Fish, remember your Pectorius.

—Epitaph of Pectorius

Dangers?

Corrupted by the evil of a lengthened peace, they (children of Israel) began to sacrifice to idols.

—Sulpitius Severus, *Sacred History*

N.B.

Thou didst touch me, and I burned for Thy peace. . . .

—Augustine, *The Confessions*

Perfection

The spirit is perfect when, thanks to real faith, it possess in super-ignorance the super-knowledge of the supremely unknowable.

—Maximus, *The Centuries on Charity*

Three important stages can be distinguished in the moral development of the monk: not to commit any sin of action; not to parley with a passionate thought; to keep peace of soul when faced with impure representations or the memory of past insults which present themselves to the mind.

—Maximus, *The Centuries on Charity*

Just as a mother is able to offer food to an infant, but the infant is not yet able to receive food unsuited to its age, so God could have offered perfection to man at the beginning, but man, being yet an infant, could not have taken it.

—Irenaeus

If then any one is aiming at perfection, from that first stage of fear which we rightly termed servile . . . he should by advancing a step to the higher path of hope—which is compared not to a slave but to a hireling, because it looks for the payment of its recompense . . . yet it cannot to that love of a son who, trusting in his father's kindness and liberality, has no doubt that all the father has is his. . . .

—John Cassian, *The First Conference of Abbot Chaeremon*

Persecution

Persecution of Christ

Thus, then, have they persecuted Him that was smitten by God, adding the pain of persecution to the pain of His wounds.

—Hilary of Poitiers, *Commentaries on the Psalms*

Persecution of Christians

You prefer to call us enemies of the human race rather than enemies of human error.

—Tertullian, *Apology*

Most grievous and painful is this persecution which arises from within, which is ever with a man, and which the persecuted cannot escape; for he carries the enemy about everywhere in himself.

—Clement of Alexandria, *Who Is the Rich Man That Shall Be Saved?*

Agents of persecution

As you have neither persecution without the injustice of the devil, nor the trial of faith without persecution, that the injustice necessary for the trial of faith does not give a warrant for persecution, but supplies an agency; that in reality, in reference to the trial of faith, which is the reason of persecution, the will of God goes first, but that as the instrument of persecution, which is the way of trial, the injustice of the devil follows.

—Tertullian, *De Fuga in Persecutione*

Nor would the devil's legion have had power over the herd of swine unless they had got it from God; so far are they from having power over the sheep of God. I may say that the bristles of the swine, too, were then counted by God, not to speak of the hairs of holy men.

—Tertullian, *De Fuga in Persecutione*

Interpretations of persecution

For what is the issue of persecution, what other result comes of it, but the approving and rejecting of faith, in regard to which the Lord will certainly sift His people? Persecution, by means of which one is declared either approved or rejected, is just the judgment of the Lord.

—Tertullian, *De Fuga in Persecutione*

This (persecution) is the fan which even now cleans the Lord's threshing floor the Church, I mean winnowing the mixed heap of believers, and separating the grain of the martyrs from the chaff of the deniers.

—Tertullian, *De Fuga in Persecutione*

Should one flee in persecution?

If persecution proceeds from God, in no way will it be our duty to flee from what has God as its author; a twofold reason opposing: for what proceeds from God ought not on the one hand to be avoided, and it cannot be evaded on the other.

—Tertullian, *De Fuga in Persecutione*

N.B.

You are deceived if you think that a Christian can live without persecution. He suffers the greatest persecution of all who lives under none.

—Jerome

Perseverance

We assert, therefore, that perseverance, by which one perseveres in Christ even to the end, is a gift of God.

—Augustine, *Gift of Perseverance*

Since no one has perseverance to the end unless he does in fact persevere to the end, many may have it, and none can lose it.

—Augustine, *Gift of Perseverance*

To be called and to be cleansed was a thing of grace. But when called and clothed in clean garments, to continue to keep those garments clean pertained to the diligence of those who are called.

—John Chrysostom, *Homilies on the Gospel of Matthew*

Poverty

But I will tell you what I think; no one can be as poor as he was born.

—Minucius Felix, *Octavius*

That man rather is poor who, though he has great possessions, desires more.

—Minucius Felix, *Octavius*

It is better for me to have no money to give away than shamelessly to beg what I mean to hoard.

—Jerome, *Letter to Nepotian*

As a man, when walking, makes the greater progress the more lightly he is burdened, so in this journey of life the man who lightens his burden by poverty is happier than one who groans beneath the weight of riches.

—Minucius Felix, *Octavius*

He is rich enough who is poor—with Christ.

—Jerome, *Letter to Heliodorus*

N.B.

Our Lord by His poverty has consecrated the poverty of His house.

—Jerome, *Letter to Nepotian*

Praise

The Christian should be an alleluia from head to foot.

—Augustine

The Seraphim who Isaiah, in the Holy Spirit, saw standing around in a circle at the throne of God . . . exclaimed, "Holy, holy, holy Lord Sabaoth." It is for this reason that we recite this theology handed down by the Seraphim: that we may be participants with the superterrestrial armies in the singing of their hymn.

—Cyril of Jerusalem, *Catechetical Lectures*

The praise of God could not be expressed in fewer words than these, "For He is good."

—Augustine, *On Psalms*

N.B.

Feigned praise is worth less than true censure.

—Clement of Alexandria, *Sermon*

Prayer

In the Name

By prayer I mean which is constantly active in the innermost secret places of the soul, so that the enemy in his secret onslaughts is invisibly flogged and scorched by calling on the name of our Lord Jesus Christ. . . .

—Hesychius of Jerusalem, *Texts on Sobriety and Prayer*

The prayer which is not made through Christ, not only cannot blot out sin, but is itself turned into sin.

—Augustine, *On the Psalms*

Privilege of prayer

May I seek you, Lord, in prayer, and believing in you, may I pray to you?

—Augustine, *Confessions*

Fasting is her (Eustochium) sport, and prayer she makes her pastime.

—Jerome, *Letter to Furia*

Power of prayer

By their prayers Christians are of more service to the realm than if they had fought for it in the legions, for by their petitions they vanquish all demons who stir up war and disturb the peace.

—Origen, *Origen's Reply to Celsus*

We are cleansed only once by baptism; by prayer we are cleansed daily.

—Augustine, *Sermon to Catechumens*

There are three things which make a shifting heart steadfast—watching, meditation, and prayer.

—John Cassian, *The Second Conference of Abbot Isaac*

For when they (Daniel, etc.) asked heavenly things from the Lord, they received also earthly things from the king.

—Hippolytus, *Commentary on Daniel*

Polishing the weapons

He who has no prayer free from thoughts has no weapon for battle.

—Hesychius of Jerusalem, *Texts on Sobriety and Prayer*

For so was Saul an enemy of the Church, for which reason prayer was offered for him, and he became her friend. Not only did he cease to be her persecutor, but he strove to be her helper. And yet if you would know the truth, prayer was not directed against him, but against his malice, that it may die out and he may live. For if your enemy were to die, it might seem that you had lost an enemy, yet you would not have found a friend. But if there is an end to his malice, you have in one stroke lost an enemy and gained a friend.

—Augustine, *The Lord's Prayer Explained*

For he prays *too little,* who is accustomed only to pray at the times when he bends his knees.

—John Cassian, *The Second Conference of Abbot Isaac*

If you are far from yourself, how can you draw near to God?

—Augustine, *Confessions*

I am on fire with innumerable and various wanderings of soul and shiftiness of heart, and cannot collect my scattered thoughts, nor can I even pour forth my prayer without interruption and images of vain figures, and the recollection of conversations and actions. . . . I feel I cannot give birth to any offspring in the shape of spiritual ideas: In order that it may be vouchsafed to me to be set free from this wretched state of mind, from which I cannot extricate myself by any number of sighs and groans, I must full surely cry out: "O God, make speed to save me: O Lord, make haste to help me."

—John Cassian, *The Second Conference of Abbot Isaac*

(Do) not give the frail body rest until the soul is fed.

—Jerome, *Letter to Eustochium*

We ought to be mindful of modesty and discipline—not to throw abroad our prayers indiscriminately, with unsubdued voices, nor to cast to God with tumultuous wordiness in a petition that ought to be commended to God by modesty; for God is the hearer, not of the voice, but of the heart.

—Cyprian, *Treatise on the Lord's Prayer*

Summit of prayer

Just as, in dying, the body separates itself from all the good things of this life, so the spirit that dies at the summit of prayer also leaves all the representations it has of the world. For without dying of that death, it is not possible to find and live with God.

—Maximus, *The Centuries on Charity*

Prayer is, after all, conversation with God.

—John Chrysostom, *Homilies on Genesis*

They converse as those who are aware that God is listening.

—Tertullian, *Apology*

Usually prayer is a question of groaning rather than speaking, tears rather than words. For He set our tears in His sight, and our groaning is not hidden from Him who made all things by His Word and does not ask for words of man.

—Augustine

The prayer of the mind is not perfect until he no longer realizes himself or the fact that he is praying.

—Anthony of Egypt

Perils of prayers

A man should be on guard against two things when he prays: to ask for something he should not ask for, and to address the petition to one who must not be invoked.

—Augustine, *The Lord's Prayer Explained*

If you desire from God the Father in heaven the death of your enemies, what do you gain? Have you not heard or read the Psalm which foretells the doom of Judas the traitor, where it is prophesied of him, "May his prayer be turned to sin"? If, then, you rise up and pray that evil may befall your enemies, your prayer will be turned to sin.

—Augustine, *The Lord's Prayer Explained*

How do you know whether he for whom today you are asking evil may not tomorrow be a better man than you.

—Augustine, *The Lord's Prayer Explained*

Prayer form

The form of his prayer is thanksgiving for the past, for the present, and for the future as already through faith present.

—Clement of Alexandria, *The Stromata*

It was our Lord who put an end to long-windedness, that you would not approach God in too many words, as though you wanted to teach God by your many words. Piety, not verbosity, is in order when you pray.

—Augustine, *The Lord's Prayer Explained*

We ought to pray often but briefly, lest if we are long about it our crafty foe may succeed in implanting something in our heart.

—John Cassian, *The Second Conference of Abbot Isaac*

(There are) different kinds of prayer, which the apostle divides in a fourfold manner. . . . "I exhort therefore first of all that supplications, prayers, intercessions, thanksgivings be made." And we cannot possibly doubt that this division was not idly made by the apostle. . . .The first seems to belong more especially to beginners, who are still troubled by the stings and recollection of their sins; the second to those who have already attained some loftiness of mind in their spiritual progress and the quest of virtue; the third to those who fulfill the completion of their vows by their works, and are so stimulated to intercede for others . . . ; the fourth to those who have already torn from their hearts the guilty thorns of conscience, and thus being now free from care can contemplate with a pure mind the beneficence of God and His compassions.

—John Cassian, *The First Conference of Abbot Isaac*

"To every one that asketh," says He; not, Everything to him that asketh. . . .

—Augustine, *Our Lord's Sermon on the Mount*

Your best servant is the one who pays less attention, when listening to you, to what is desired and more to what is heard.

—Augustine, *Confessions*

Old-world prayer, indeed, used to free from fires, and from beasts, and from famine; and yet it had not (then) received its form from Christ. But how far more amply operative is *Christian* prayer! It does not station the angel of dew in mid-fires, nor muzzle lions, nor transfer to the hungry the rustics' bread; it has no delegated grace to avert any sense of suffering; but it supplies the suffering, and the feeling and the grieving, with endurance: it amplifies grace by virtue, that faith may know what she obtains from the Lord, understanding what for God's name's sake—she suffers.

—Tertullian, *On Prayer*

Unity of prayer

If the prayer of one or two possesses such power that Christ stands in the midst of them, how much more will the prayer of the bishop and of the whole Church, ascending up in harmony to God, prevail for the granting of all their petitions in Christ!

—Ignatius, *Epistle to the Ephesians*

He also prays in the society of angels, as being already of angelic rank, and he is never out of their angelic keeping; and though he pray alone, he has the choir of the saints standing with him.

—Clement of Alexandria, *The Stromata*

⇴ Divine prompting

The nature of the divine goodness is not only to open to those who knock, but also to *cause them* to knock and ask.

—Augustine

⇴ If God already knows, why ask?

Is He unable, then, to present His gifts without our asking? It is for this reason that He waits: so that He may have occasion from us of justly making us worthy of His providential care.

—John Chrysostom, *Homilies on Genesis*

⇴ Lord's prayer

What praying to the Father can be more truthful than that which was delivered to us by the Son who is the Truth, out of His own mouth? So that to pray otherwise than He taught is not ignorance alone, but also sin. . . .

—Cyprian, *Treatise on the Lord's Prayer*

It is a loving and friendly prayer to beseech God with His own word, to come up to His ears in the prayer of Christ. Let the Father acknowledge the words of His Son when we make our prayer, and let Him also who dwells within in our breast Himself dwell in our voice.

—Cyprian, *Treatise on the Lord's Prayer*

How much more effectually do we obtain what we ask in Christ's name, if we ask for it in His own prayer!

—Cyprian, *Treatise on the Lord's Prayer*

⇴ N.B.

Feed prayers on fasting.

—Tertullian, *Repentance*

Preaching

Dogma and kerygma

Dogma and kerygma are two distinct things. Dogma is observed in silence; kerygma is proclaimed to all the world.

—Basil the Great, *The Holy Spirit*

Do's and don'ts

For this reason too the prophets were called seers, because they saw Him who others did not see.

—Jerome, *Letter to Paulinus*

. . . for a table with only one sort of food produces a satiety, while variety provokes the appetite.

—John Chrysostom

The very food without which it is impossible to live must be flavored to meet the tastes of the majority.

—Augustine

For too great length in a sermon is as much an enemy to people's ears, as too much food is to their bodies. . . .

—Gregory of Nazianzus, *Oration on Holy Baptism*

A man speaks more or less wisely in proportion as he makes more or less progress in the Holy Scriptures.

—Augustine

(Those) that are ordained at the present day from among the literate class make it their study not how to seek out the marrow of Scripture, but how to tickle the ears of the people with the flowers of rhetoric.

—Jerome, *The Dialogue Against the Luciferians*

For just as the speaker is pleasing when he makes clear things which should be learned, so he is irksome when he keeps emphasizing facts already known.

—Augustine

We preachers humour fancies instead of trying to crush them. We act like a father who gives his sick child a cake or an ice, or something else that is merely nice to eat—just because he asks for it; and takes no pains to give him what is good for him; and when the doctors blame him says, "I could not bear to hear my child cry." . . . This is what we do when we elaborate beautiful sentences, fine combinations and harmonies, to please and not to profit. . . .

—John Chrysostom, *Homilies on Acts*

He helps his hearers more by his wisdom than his oratory; although he himself is less useful than he would be if he were an eloquent speaker also. But the one to guard against is the man whose eloquence is no more than an abundant flow of empty words.

—Augustine, *De Doctrina Christiana*

The Grand Design

My mother went to church twice a day; she went in the morning and evening without ever allowing anything to keep her away, and she went not to hear idle tales and the gossip of old women, but that she might hear Thee, O Lord, in Thy sermons, and that Thou might hear her in her prayers.

—Augustine, *Confessions*

N.B.

I know that a difference must be made between the apostles and all other preachers. The former always speak the truth; but the latter being men sometimes go astray.

—Jerome, *Letter to Theophilus Bishop of Alexandria*

Preaching makes me well; as soon as I open my mouth to speak, all my weariness is forgotten.

—John Chrysostom

Pride

(See also: Selfishness)

Potency of pride

He had made two kinds of creatures to know Him, to wit, the angelic and the human. Pride shattered each of them.

—Gregory the Great, *Moral Teaching from Job*

And he (Hezekiah) who by a single prayer of his was able to procure the death of a hundred and eighty-five thousand of the army of the Assyrians . . . is overcome by boasting and vanity.

—John Cassian, *Of the Spirit of Vainglory*

How great is the evil of pride, that it rightly has no angel, nor other virtues opposed to it, but God Himself as its adversary!

—John Cassian, *The Institutes*

Pride is the cause and fountain head of evils. . . .

—John Cassian, *The Institutes*

Pride is the beginning of sin, the first impulse and movement toward evil.

—John Chrysostom, *Homilies on Thessalonians*

There are times when we are even more overcome by pride than the pagan princes, worldly and wicked though they are, and we all but give ourselves bodyguards, like kings. We terrify people and make ourselves inaccessible especially if they are poor. . . . You can see this happen in many a well-known church, especially in the big cities.

—Origen, *Commentary on Matthew*

Tactics of pride

The demon of pride has two tactics: either he suggests the attribution to oneself of good work, instead of attributing it to God. . . . Or else, if the monk turn a deaf ear, the demon inspires him with contempt for his still imperfect brothers.

—Maximus, *The Centuries on Charity*

Nor does this malady endeavour to wound a man except through his virtues.

—John Cassian, *Of the Spirit of Vainglory*

If he (Satan) cannot make him puffed up by the grace of knowledge and eloquence, he pulls him down by the weight of silence.

—John Cassian, *Of the Spirit of Vainglory*

What use is the robe of a penitent if it covers the pride of a king?

—Jerome, *Letter to the Presbyter Marcus*

All men fall into this (pride) who are in a moment made masters, actually before they are disciples.

—Jerome, *Letter to Oceanus*

Distinctives

You can tell a man's inward condition from his outward gait.

—John Cassian, *The Institutes*

By these signs, then . . . carnal pride . . . is shown. To begin with, in conversation the man's voice is loud: in his silence there is bitterness: in his mirth his laughter is noisy and excessive: when he is serious he is unreasonably gloomy: in his answers there is rancour: he is too free with his tongue, his words tumbling out at random without being weighed. . . .

—John Cassian, *The Institutes*

Remedy

God . . . has been careful to heal opposites with opposites, that those things which were ruined by pride might be restored by humility.

—John Cassian, *The Institutes*

N.B.

I should prefer no good to a vain good.

—Tertullian, *On Modesty*

Prophecy

(See also: Eschatology; Second Coming)

The Jewish nation, condemned for unbelief, is rooted out of its own land and dispersed through every region of the world that it might carry everywhere the Sacred Scriptures, and that the testimony of the prophecies by which Christ and the Church were foretold might be furnished by our adversaries, so that it could not be thought that these predictions had been forged by us. . . .

—Augustine, *Letter to Marcellinus*

Certainty of fulfillment

For the things concerning Christ are all put into writing, and nothing is doubtful, for nothing is without a text. All are inscribed on the monuments of the prophets; clearly written, not on tablets of stone, but by the Holy Ghost. Since then thou hast heard the Gospel speaking concerning Judas, oughtest thou not to receive the testimony to it? Thou hast heard that He was pierced in the side by a spear; oughtest thou not to see whether this also is written? Thou hast heard that He was crucified in a garden; oughtest thou not to see whether this also is written? Thou hast heard that He was sold for thirty pieces of silver; oughtest thou not to learn what prophet spake this? Thou hast heard that He was given vinegar to drink; learn where this also is written. Thou hast heard that His body was laid in a rock, and that a stone was set over it; oughtest thou not to receive this testimony also from the prophet? Thou hast heard that He was crucified with robbers; oughtest thou not see whether this also is written? Thou hast heard that He was buried; oughtest thou not to see whether the circumstances of His burial are anywhere accurately written? Thou hast heard that He rose again; oughtest thou not to see whether we mock thee in teaching these things?

—Cyril of Jerusalem, *Catechetical Lectures*

All these things are now seen to be fulfilled in accordance with the predictions which we read; and these fulfillments are now so many and so great that they lead us to await with confidence fulfillment of the rest.

—Augustine, *Letter to Marcellinus*

Since all things which have happened were predicted before they occurred, we should trust that similar prophecies, which are not yet fulfilled, will quite certainly happen. The prophecies already fulfilled came true even though they were not understood. In the same way the other prophecies will also quite certainly come true, even though they are not understood and not believed.

—Justin, *The First Apology*

Therefore we ought to give most fervent thanks to the Lord for making known to us the past, for giving us light about the present, and for not leaving us without discernment of the future.

—Ignatius, *Letter to Polycarp*

Why should we believe a crucified man, that He is the First-born of the unbegotten God, and that He will pass judgment on the whole human race, if we had not found testimonies published about Him before He came and was made man, and if we had not seen these predictions fulfilled?

—Justin, *The First Apology*

Can a false prophet speak the truth?

Some true words he does occasionally utter; for the devil fills him with his own spirit, in the hope that he may be able to overcome some of the righteous.

—Hermas, *The Shepherd*

Test the prophets

Not every man who speaks in the Spirit is a prophet, but only if he has the manner of the Lord. Thus the false and the true prophet shall be known by their manner of life. . . . Further, every prophet who teaches the truth is a false prophet if he does not do what he teaches.

—Didache

Does prediction bring on calamities?

"It is impossible that scandals should not come." . . . It is not that His prediction brings the scandals. Away with such a notion! It is not because He foretold it that it happens; but because it surely must happen He did foretell it.

—John Chrysostom, *Homilies on the Gospel of Matthew*

A threefold testimony, also a fourth

Some ignorantly deny Him, or rather have been denied by Him, being the advocates of death rather than of the truth. These persons neither have the prophets persuaded, nor the law of Moses, nor the Gospel even to this day, nor the sufferings we have individually endured.

—Ignatius, *Epistle to the Smyrneans*

When shall this be?

For in as many days as this world was made, in so many thousand years shall it be concluded. And for this reason the Scripture says: "Thus the heaven and the earth were finished, and all their adornment. And God brought to a conclusion upon the sixth day the works that He had made; and God rested upon the seventh day from all His works." This is an account of the things formerly created, as also it is a prophecy of what is to come.

—Irenaeus, *Against Heresies*

Now it did not say that it (the stone) smote upon the head of the image, nor on its breast and arms, nor yet on its belly and thighs, but on its feet; because that, of the whole image, that stone when it comes will find the feet alone.

—Aphrahat, *Select Demonstrations*

N.B.

We pray for the postponement of the end.

—Tertullian, *Apology*

Punishment

Punishment, that is the justice of the unjust.

—Augustine

Sins which are punished by an extremely lengthy period of penalties are committed in an extremely short time. . . .

—Augustine, *The City of God*

The only payment that is owed us is punishment.

—Augustine, *Psalms*

Here or hereafter?

For if every sin were now visited with manifest punishment, nothing would seem to be reserved for the final judgment; on the other hand, if no sin received now a plainly divine punishment, it would be concluded that there is no divine providence at all.

—Augustine, *The City of God*

Why the delay?

God, whose judgment the slower it is the juster it is. . . .

—Minucius Felix, *Octavius*

Agents of punishment?

Such of our brethren as transgress, we must not punish, but rebuke.

—Clement of Alexandria, *The Instructor*

Degrees of punishment?

In regard to punishment, I say that not all men are equal. He that sins much is much tormented. He that offended not so much is less tormented.

—Aphraates, *Treatises*

After the resurrection . . . both the joy of the good will be greater and the torments of the wicked more severe, when they will be tortured along with their body. . . .

—Augustine, *Homilies on John*

What sort a punishment, and how great, is due to each fault, belongs to divine judgment, not to human; which punishment assuredly when it is remitted in the case of the converted, there is great goodness on the part of God; and when it is deservedly inflicted, there is no injustice on the part of God.

—Augustine, *The Nature of the Good*

The curse of going unpunished

He must be reckoned the most unfortunate of men, who, while living unrighteously, remains for a long time unpunished.

—Justin Martyr, quoted by Antonius Melissa

The ultimate

For there is no greater or worse death than when death never dies.

—Augustine, *The City of God*

Souls in punishment will seek death. They prefer not to be rather than to be punished. It is for this they shall seek death and not find it.

—Origen, *On the Soul*

"The voice of the Lord divides the flame of fire" (Psalm 29:7). . . . I believe that the fire prepared in punishment for the devil and his angels is divided by the voice of the Lord. Thus, since there are two capacities in fire, one of burning and the other of illuminating, the fierce and punitive property of the fire may await those who deserve to burn, while its illuminating and radiant part may be reserved for the enjoyment of those who are rejoicing.

—Basil the Great, *Homilies on the Psalms*

There are venial sins and there are mortal sins. It is one thing to owe ten thousand talents, another to owe but a farthing. We shall have to give an accounting for an idle word no less than for adultery. . . . There is a great difference between one sin and another.

—Jerome, *Against Jovinian*

But there is one form of punishment peculiar to man—the death of the body.

—Augustine, *Enchiridion*

Do the good and the bad suffer equally?

Though good and bad men suffer alike, we must not suppose that there is no difference between the men themselves, because there is no difference in what they both suffer. For even in the likeness of the sufferings, there remains an unlikeness in the sufferers.

—Augustine, *The City of God*

If a man is sinful, he shall receive an eternal body fitted to endure the penalties of sin, so that he may burn in the eternal fire without ever being consumed.

—Cyril of Jerusalem, *Catechetical Lectures*

Eternal punishment?

If . . . there were going to be an end of eternal punishment, there would likewise be an end to eternal life.

—Basil the Great, *Rules Briefly Treated*

No sleep will give them rest; no night will soothe them; no death will deliver them from punishment; no appeal of interceding friends will profit them.

—Hippolytus, *Against the Greeks*

There is punishment, deathless, unallayed, and no one to stand up for us.

—John Chrysostom, *Homilies on Thessalonians*

Be your own prosecutor and judge

Since . . . sin must not go unpunished, let it be punished by you, lest you be punished for it. Let your sin have you for its judge, not its patron.

—Augustine, *Psalms*

Purity

When recently you condemned a Christian maiden to a panderer rather than to a panther, you realized and confessed openly that with us a stain on our purity is regarded as more dreadful than any punishment and worse than death.

—Tertullian, *Apology*

What is pure is corrupted much more quickly than what is corrupt is purified.

—John Cassian, *The First Conference of Abbot Nesteros*

The old enemy knows that the battle with impurity is a harder one than that with covetousness. It is easy to cast off what clings to us from without, but a war within our borders involves far greater peril.

—Jerome, *Letter to Tranquillinus*

Reason

(See also: Intellect; Mind)

God-made

Far be it from God to hate in us that faculty by which He made us so much more excellent than the other living creatures.

—Augustine, *Letter to Consentius*

Reason, in fact, is a thing of God, inasmuch as there is nothing which God the Maker of all has not provided, disposed, ordained by reason—nothing which He has not willed should be handled and understood by reason.

—Tertullian, *On Repentance*

Casualty of the fall?

In some points, then, that pertain to the salvific doctrine, which we can not yet grasp by reason, —though some day we shall—let reason be preceded by faith, which cleanses the heart, so that the heart may receive and retain the light of great reason; and this too is reasonable.

—Augustine, *Letter to Consentius*

There is, if I do not err, just and ample reason; but I do not demand a reason of Christ. If I am convinced by reason, I am rejecting faith.

—Ambrose of Milan, *The Death of His Brother Satyrus*

N.B.

For though the soul may seem to rule the body admirably, and the reason the vices, if the soul and reason do not themselves obey God, as God has commanded them to serve Him, they have no proper authority over the body and the vices.

—Augustine, *City of God*

Repentance

Marks of repentance

He who beats his heart, but does not mend his ways, does not remove his sins but hardens them.

—Augustine

For there is nothing more destructive of sin than (self) accusation and (self) condemnation, joined to repentance and tears.

—John Chrysostom, *Homilies Against the Anomoians*

Where there is no fear, in like manner there is no amendment; where there is no amendment, repentance is of necessity vain.

—Tertullian, *On Repentance*

Power of repentance

Some are of the mind that the only ones who sin against the Holy Spirit are those who, after they have been washed in the bath of rebirth in the Church and have accepted the Holy Spirit, have afterwards plunged themselves . . . into some death-dealing sin. . . . But how this meaning could be shown, I do not know, since in the Church there is no denial of a place of repentance for any crime whatsoever.

—Augustine, *Sermons*

Even if you are in extreme old age and have sinned, go in, repent! For here there is a physician's office, not a courtroom; not a place where punishment of sin is exacted, but where the forgiveness of sin is granted.

—John Chrysostom, *Homilies Against the Anomoians*

Take heed lest without reason thou mistrust the power of repentance. Wouldst thou know what power repentance has? . . . Hezekiah by means of confession routed a hundred and fourscore and five thousand of his enemies. A great thing verily was this, but still small in comparison with what remains to be told: the same king by repentance obtained the recall of a divine sentence which had already gone forth.

—Cyril of Jerusalem, *Catechetical Lectures*

What if I sin again?

As often as you might fall down in the marketplace, you pick yourself up again. So too, as often as you sin, repent your sin. Do not despair. Even if you sin a second time, repent a second time.

—John Chrysostom, *Homilies Against the Anomoians*

To him who still remains in this world there is no repentance that is too late.

—Cyprian, *To Demetrian*

Medicine must be repeated for a repeated sickness.

—Tertullian, *Repentance*

The shame involved?

Let us . . . imitate the (Samaritan) woman, and in the face of our own sins not be ashamed because of men. Rather, as is proper, let us fear God who sees now what we have done and who punishes later what we do not repent now. At present we do the opposite of this. Instead of fearing Him who is to judge us, we shudder at those who in no way hurt us, and we tremble at the shame which comes from them.

—John Chrysostom, *Homilies on the Gospel of John*

The human race is curious to know about other people's lives but lazy in correcting its own.

—Augustine, *Confessions*

If he does not want them (his sins) to be paraded on that fearful day, let him apply now the medicines of repentance and let him heal now his wounds.

—John Chrysostom, *Homilies on the Gospel of John*

Satisfactions?

Peter was sorrowful and he wept because, being a man, he has strayed. I do not find that he said anything; but I do find he wept. I read about his tears, but I do not read about any satisfaction. But what cannot be defended can be washed away.

—Ambrose of Milan, *Commentary on the Gospel of Luke*

Caution

Thus he who, through repentance for sins, had begun to make satisfaction to the Lord, will, through another repentance of his repentance, make satisfaction to the devil, and will be the more hateful to God in proportion as he will be the more acceptable to His rival.

—Tertullian, *On Repentance*

Though after this life repentance be perpetual, it is in vain.

—Augustine

N.B.

"Is it good to repent, or no?" Why do you ponder? God enjoins; nay, He not merely enjoins, but likewise exhorts. He invites by reward—salvation, to wit; even by an oath, saying "As I live." He desires that credence may be given Him. Oh blessed we, for whose sake God swears! Oh most miserable, if we believe not the Lord even when He swears! What, therefore, God so highly commends, what He even attests on oath, we are bound, of course, to approach, and to guard with the utmost seriousness; that, abiding permanently in the solemn pledge of divine grace, we may be able also to persevere in like manner in its fruit and its benefit.

—Tertullian, *On Repentance*

Reproving

Definitions

Reproof and rebuke . . . are the stripes of the soul, chastising sins, preventing death, and leading to self-control those carried away to licentiousness.

—Clement of Alexandria, *The Instructor*

Reproof is, as it were, the surgery of the passions of the soul; and the passions are, as it were, an abscess of the truth, which must be cut open by an incision of the lancet of reproof.

—Clement of Alexandria, *The Instructor*

Guidelines

For he who wants to heal another's wound ought to be in good health and free from every affection of weakness himself.

—John Cassian, *Of the Spirit of Anger*

As the mirror is not evil to an ugly man because it shows him what he is like; and as the physician is not evil to the sick man because he tells him of his fever, so neither is he, that reproves, ill-disposed towards him who is diseased in the soul.

—Clement of Alexandria, *The Instructor*

He, then, who perceives any evil in his neighbour, and keeps silent about it, acts like the surgeon who looks at his friend's wound and will not cure it.

—Gregory the Great, *Pastoral Care*

His (Eli) reproofs were too gentle to serve the purpose of discipline.

—Sulpitius Severus, *Sacred History*

He who soothes the sinner with flattering blandishments furnishes the stimulus to sin; nor does he repress; but nourishes wrong-doing.

—Cyprian, *On the Unity of the Church*

What if the reprover is young?

Daniel the wise, at twelve years of age, became possessed of the Divine Spirit, and convicted the elders, who in vain carried their gray hairs, of being false accusers.... Samuel also, when he was but a child, reproved Eli, who was ninety years old, for giving honour to his sons rather than to God.... Wherefore youth is not to be despised when it is devoted to God. But he is to be despised who is of a wicked mind, although he be old, and full of wicked days. Timothy the Christ-bearer was young, but hear what his teacher writes to him: "Let no man despise thy youth."

—Ignatius, *Epistle to the Magnesians*

Rest

Thou hast formed us for Thyself, and our hearts are restless till they find their rest in Thee.

—Augustine, *Confessions*

Eternal rest awaits those who have struggled through the present life observant of the laws, not as payment owed for their works, but bestowed as a gift of the munificent God on those who have hoped in Him.

—Basil the Great, *Homilies on the Psalms*

I have learned from experience that the ass toiling along the highway makes for an inn when it is weary.

—Jerome, *Letter to Laeta*

Resurrection

Analogies

Day and night show us the resurrection: night goes to rest, day breaks in; day departs, night comes on.

—Clement, *Letter to the Corinthians*

Consider the crops. How and in what manner does sowing take place? The farmer goes out and casts all the seeds on the soil: they are dry and bare; they fall on the soil: they decay. After they have decayed, the Lord's sublime providence raises them up.

—Clement, *Letter to the Corinthians*

All nature suggests the future resurrection. The sun sinks down, but is reborn. The stars go out, but return again. Flowers die, but come to life again. After their decay shrubs put forth leaves again; not unless seeds decay does their strength return. A body in the grave is like the trees in winter: they hide their sap under a deceptive dryness. Why are you in haste for it to revive and return, while yet the winter is raw? We must await even the spring of the body.

—Minucius Felix, *Octavius*

For like the seeds which are cast into the earth, we do not perish by dissolution, but sown in the earth, shall rise again, death having been brought to nought by the grace of the Saviour. Hence it is that blessed Paul, who was made a surety of the Resurrection to all, says: "This corruptible must put on incorruption, and this mortal must put on immortality. . . ."

—Athanasius, *Incarnation of the Word*

Is it not absurd, that which has been produced with such circumstance, and which is beyond all else valuable, should be so neglected by its Maker, as to pass to nonentity? Then the sculptor and painter, if they wish the works they have made to endure, that they may win glory by them, renew them when they begin to decay; but God would so neglect His own possession and work, that it becomes annihilated, and no longer exists. Should we not call this labour in vain?

—Justin, *On the Resurrection*

Declarations

God did not create man in a purposeless enterprise.

—Athenagoras of Athens, *The Resurrection of the Dead*

The linkage of all conditions and activities must relate to some unified goal. The origin and nature of man, his living, doing, and suffering, the whole course of his earthly existence, and the end befitting his nature—all these must become one, must find harmony, unity, and complete accord throughout his being.

—Athenagoras, *On the Resurrection of the Dead*

He accepted a decaying body so that decaying bodies might put on immortality.

—Athanasius, *Resurrection Letters VIII*

The Word recognizes three births for us; namely, the natural birth, that of baptism, and that of the resurrection.

—Gregory of Nazianaus, *Oration on Holy Baptism*

An array of arguments

If Christ died and did not rise how is it that those in the account who fled from impending danger while He was yet alive, surrounded themselves with a thousand dangers for His sake when He was dead?

—John Chrysostom, *Homilies on the Beginning of the Acts of the Apostles*

And surely He that created is competent to recreate, since it is a much greater thing to produce than it is to reproduce.

—Tertullian, *The Resurrection of the Dead*

It is more difficult to initiate that which is not, than to repeat that which has been.

—Minucius Felix, *Octavius*

If earth and heaven are renewed, why should we doubt that man can be renewed, when it is on his account that earth and heaven were made?

—Ambrose of Milan, *The Death of His Brother Satyrus*

If, when Adam did not exist, He made him from nothing, how much easier will it now be for Him to raise him up.

—Aphraates, *Treatises*

⇼ Resurrection of the body

The resurrection is a resurrection of the flesh which died. For the spirit dies not; the soul is in the body, and without a soul it cannot live. The body when the soul forsakes it, is not. For the body is the house of the soul; and the soul the house of the spirit. These three, in all those who cherish the sincere hope and unquestioning faith in God, will be saved.

—Justin, *On the Resurrection*

The salvation of the soul would be the final goal of only a part of the human being, not of the whole. In order that the final goal can be realized, the body must be united with the soul, which is possible only through resurrection.

—Athenagoras, *On the Resurrection of the Dead*

If He (Christ) had no need of the flesh, why did He heal it?

—Justin, *On the Resurrection*

We therefore have formed the belief that (our) bodies also do rise again. For although they go to corruption, yet they do not perish; for the earth, receiving the remains, preserves them, even like fertile seed mixed with more fertile ground.

—Irenaeus, *Fragments from Lost Writings*

If Christ, the Lord who saved us, though He was originally spirit, became flesh and in this state called us, so also shall we receive our reward in the flesh.

—Clement of Rome, *Second Letter to the Corinthians*

Do you think that if something be withdrawn from our feeble eyes, it perishes to God? Everybody, whether it withers into dust or is dissolved into moisture or is crumbled into ashes or passes off as a vapour, is removed from our eyes; but a guard is kept over its elements by God.

—Minucius Felix, *Octavius*

If God produced all things out of nothing, He will also be able to draw forth from nothing the flesh which has fallen into nothing.

—Tertullian, *The Resurrection of the Dead*

What is that which died? Was it not a body? It is of the body, then, that there will be a resurrection.

—Origen, *De Principiis*

We do nothing without the body. We blaspheme with the mouth; with the mouth we pray. We fornicate with the body; with the body we are chaste. We rob with the hand; with the hand we bestow alms. . . . Since in all things the body has been our agent, it too shall in the future share in the fruits of what has been done.

—Cyril of Jerusalem, *Catechetical Lectures*

. . . the Lord Jesus exhorting His martyrs to patience, hath promised to the very body a future perfect entireness, without loss; I say not of any limb, but of a single hair.

—Augustine, *On Patience*

A potpourri of arguments

What if the body be deformed or destroyed?

(The unbelievers say) if then the flesh rise, it must rise the same as it falls; so that if it die with one eye, it must rise one-eyed; if lame, lame; if defective in any part of the body, in this part the man must rise deficient. How truly blinded are they in the eyes of their hearts! For they have not seen on the earth blind men seeing again, and the lame walking by His word. All things which the Saviour did, He did in the first place (to fulfill the prophecies) . . . but also to induce the belief that in the resurrection the flesh shall rise entire. For if on earth He healed the sicknesses of the flesh and made the body whole, much more will He do this in the resurrection, so that the flesh shall rise perfect and entire.

—Justin, *On the Resurrection*

Even though the body has been all quite ground to powder by some severe accident or by the ruthlessness of enemies, and though it has been so diligently scattered to the winds or into the water that there is no trace of it left, yet it shall not be beyond the omnipotence of the Creator—no, not a hair of its head shall perish. The flesh shall then be spiritual and subject to the spirit, but still flesh not spirit, as the spirit itself, when subject to the flesh, was fleshly but still spirit and not flesh.

—Augustine, *City of God*

But is not the flesh contemptible?

Considering how vile and despicable the flesh is, is it not vile (they claim) that God should raise it . . . it is not worthy of the resurrection. . . .

"And God took dust of the earth, and made man." It is evident, therefore, that man made in the image of God was of flesh. Is it not then, absurd to say, that the flesh made by God in His own image is contemptible, worth nothing?

—Justin, *On the Resurrection*

But doesn't the body cause the soul to sin?

(They say) the flesh is a sinner, so much so, that it forces the soul to sin along with it. . . .

But in what instance can the flesh possibly sin by itself, if it have not the soul going before it and inciting it? For as in the case of a yoke of oxen, if one or other is loosed from the yoke, neither of them can plough alone; so neither can soul or body alone effect anything, if they be unyoked from their communion.

—Justin, *On the Resurrection*

⇔ Where is the promise of the resurrection of the flesh?

Where He promises to save man, there He gives the promise to the flesh. For what is man but the reasonable animal composed of body and soul? Is the soul by itself man? No; but the soul of man. Would the body be called man? No, but it is called the body of man. If, then, neither of these is by itself man, but that which is made up of the two together is called man, and God has called *man* to life and resurrection, He has called not a part, but the whole, which is the soul and the body.

—Justin, *On the Resurrection*

⇔ What of the wicked?

There will be a resurrection even of the wicked, but without the change which God is going to give to the faithful alone. . . .

—Fulgence of Ruspe, *The Rule of Faith*

⇔ Going for the jugular!

But you do not believe that the dead are raised. When the resurrection shall take place, then you will believe, whether you will or not; and your faith shall be reckoned for unbelief, unless you believe now.

—Theophilus of Antioch, *To Autolycus*

Whoever . . . says that there is neither resurrection nor judgment, such a one is the first-born of Satan.

—Polycarp, *Letter to the Philippians*

⇔ Death has a word

Gluttonous Death, lamented and said, I have learned fasting, which I used not to know; lo! Jesus gathers multitudes, but as to me, in His feast a fast is proclaimed for me. One man has closed a mouth, mine who have closed the mouths of many. . . . This Man triumphs. . . . He changes the vesture of the dead into life.

—Ephraim the Syrian, *Nisibene Hymns*

N.B.

It is unbelievable that the world should have believed so unbelievable a thing.

—Augustine, *The City of God*

Revenge

The precept, "Resist not evil," was given to prevent us from taking revenge . . . but not to make us neglect the duty of restraining men from sin.

—Augustine, *To Publicola*

Do you not see how the bee dies upon the sting? By that animal God instructs us not to grieve our neighbours. For we ourselves receive death first.

—John Chrysostom, *Homilies on Thessalonians*

Remedy?

Do you not see in houses, when two doors stand directly opposite, and there is a strong wind, if you shut one, and there is no opposite draught, the wind has no power, but the greater part of its force is abated? So also now, there are two doors, thy mouth, and his who insults and affronts thee; if thou shuttest thy mouth, and dost not allow a draught on the other side, thou hast quenched the whole blast; but if thou openest it, it will not be restrained.

—John Chrysostom, *Homilies on Thessalonians*

Rewards

We remind you rather to hope for reward, than look for pardon.

—Sulpitius Severus, *Letter to Claudia*

The root of every good work is the hope of the resurrection; for the expectation of a reward nerves the soul to good work.

—Cyril of Jerusalem, *Catechetical Lectures*

Where the battle is hard, the crown of victory is all the more glorious.

—Sulpitius Severus, *Letter to Claudia*

You are running for yourself; see to your own interests.

—Cyril of Jerusalem, *Catechetical Letters*

Degrees of rewards?

The denarius which the householder orders to be given to all of those who worked in his vineyard, with no distinction between those who labored less and those who labored more, is given equally to all. By that denarius it is certainly eternal life that is signified, in which no one lives longer than anyone else, since in eternity life has no diversity in its measure. But the many mansions signify different worth of merits in the one eternal life.

—Augustine, *Homilies on John*

Know then, that even when the sons of men shall enter into life, still, reward shall exceed reward, and glory shall exceed glory, and recompense shall be greater than recompense.

—Aphraates, *Treatises*

If you have labored little, you will receive little; but if your labor has been great, great will be your reward.

—Cyril of Jerusalem, *Catechetical Letter*

It is our task, according to our different virtues, to prepare for ourselves different rewards. . . . If we were all going to be equal in heaven it would be useless for us to humble ourselves here in order to have a greater place there. . . . Why should virgins persevere? Why should widows toil? Why should married women be continent? Let us all sin, and after we repent we shall be the same as the apostles are!

—Jerome, *Against Jovinian*

Look ahead

For in this life, though holy men and holy pursuits afford us great consolations, yet the blessings which men crave are not invariably bestowed upon them, lest religion should be cultivated for the sake of these temporal advantages, while it ought rather to be cultivated for the sake of that other life from which all evil is excluded.

—Augustine, *City of God*

N.B.

For nothing could perish on earth save what they would be ashamed to carry away from earth.

—Augustine, *City of God*

Riches

Riches and the desire of wealth is a drunkeness of the soul. . . .

—John Chrysostom, *Homilies on Thessalonians*

What he (the apostle) blames in riches is not the possession of them, but the desire of them.

—Augustine, *The City of God*

His wealth need not stand in the way of the rich man, if he makes a good use of it; and poverty can be no recommendation to the poor if in the midst of squalor and want he fails to keep clear of wrong doing.

—Jerome, *Letter to Salvina*

There is no fault to be found with money: but whenever thou hast made a bad use of that which is good, then being unwilling to blame thine own management, thou impiously throwest back the blame upon the Creator.

—Cyril of Jerusalem, *Lecture VIII*

The poverty of riches

Earthly riches are full of poverty.

—Augustine

No matter how rich one may be on earth, one is still God's beggar. . . . Have not many lain down to sleep as wealthy men, and risen up as paupers?

—Augustine, *The Lord's Prayer Explained*

When there is a chance of saving money we quicken our pace, speak promptly, and keep our ears open. . . . The gain of a penny fills with joy; the loss of a half-penny plunges us into sorrow.

—Jerome, *Letter to Marcella*

The curse of riches

The lust which commits fornication with gold becomes an idol.

—Clement of Alexandria, *The Instructor*

Those who could not be injured by adversity are ruined, unless they are careful by prosperity; and those who in the conflict of battle have escaped the danger of death fall before their own trophies and triumphs.

—John Cassian, *Of the Spirit of Vainglory*

Their possession amounts to this only, that they can keep others from possessing it; and oh, what a marvellous perversion of names! They call those things *goods*, which they absolutely put to none but *bad* uses.

—Cyprian, *Epistles*

It is the glory of a bishop to make provision for the wants of the poor; but it is the shame of all priests to amass private fortunes.

—Jerome, *Letter to Nepotian*

If a man talks to you always or nearly always about money . . . treat him as a broker rather than a monk.

—Jerome, *Letter to Paulinus*

The bondage of riches

He does not see, poor wretch, that his life is but a gilded torture, that he is bound fast by his wealth, and that his money owns him rather than he own it.

—Cyprian, *Epistles*

The higher ground

Your purse ought not to remain full while I am in need.

—Jerome, *Letter to Nepotian*

It is necessary that the eye of the ruler be not obscured by the dust of earthly cares.

—Gregory the Great, *Pastoral Care*

Show forth all your wealth in giving.

—Commodianus, *Instructions*

We prefer to despise wealth than to possess it.

—Minucius Felix, *Octavius*

The true riches

It is not he who has and keeps, but he who gives away, that is rich.

—Clement of Alexandria, *The Instructor*

How can anyone be considered poor who does not feel any want, who does not covet what belongs to others, who is rich in God's eyes?

—Minicius Felix, *Octavius*

This visible appearance cheats death and the devil; for the wealth within, the beauty, is unseen by them. And they rave about the carcase, which they despise as weak, being blind to the wealth within; knowing not what a "treasure in an earthen vessel" we bear, protected as it is by the power of God the Father, and the blood of God the Son, and the dew of the Holy Spirit.

—Clement of Alexandria, *Who Is the Rich Man That Shall Be Saved?*

As the fabric of the world totters, let us quickly transfer our treasure to a world which will know no shock.

—Augustine

To go about without a linen scarf on is nothing; what is praiseworthy is to be without money to buy one.

—Jerome, *Letter to Nepotian*

The best riches

The best riches is poverty of desires.

—Clement of Alexandria, *The Instructor*

Nothing that is God's is obtainable by money.

—Tertullian

Gold, even though you desire it, you may perhaps never possess; God you will possess as soon as you desire Him.

—Augustine, *On Psalms*

N.B.

Why do we cherish and love what is Peter's boast not to possess?

—Jerome, *Letter to Nepotian*

Righteousness

Righteousness, then, is nothing else than not to commit sin; and not to commit sin is just to keep the precepts of the law. Now, the observance of these precepts is maintained in a twofold way—thus, that one do none of those things which are forbidden, and that he strive to fulfill the things which are commanded.

—Sulpitius Severus, *Letter to Claudia*

The trangression of sinners was not so great as the righteousness of Him that died for them.

—Cyril of Jerusalem, *Catechetical Lectures*

I perceived and found it nothing strange that bread which is pleasant to a healthy palate is loathsome to one distempered: and to sore eyes light is offensive, which to the sound is delightful. And Thy righteousness displeaseth the wicked. . . .

—Augustine, *Confessions*

Rumors

Gehenna itself bubbles up in hell with rumours.

—Commodianus, *Instructions*

A fire of straw quickly dies out and a spreading flame soon expires if fuel to it be wanting.

—Jerome, *Letter to Furia*

For it is not lawful for you patiently to listen to evil-speaking against another, inasmuch as you would not wish that to be done by others when directed against yourself.

—Sulpitius Severus, *Letter to Claudia*

Salvation

(See also: Second Birth)

Of the Lord

There can be no doubt that all who actually come to the knowledge of the truth and to salvation do so not in virtue of their own merits but of the efficacious help of Divine Grace.

—Prosper of Aquitaine, *The Call of All Nations*

We therefore, who have been called by His will in Christ Jesus, are not justified by ourselves, neither by our wisdom or understanding or piety, not by the works we have wrought in holiness of heart, but by the faith by which almighty God has justified all men from the beginning.

—Clement of Rome, *Letter to the Corinthians*

God does many good things in man which man does not do; but man does none which God does not cause man to do.

—Augustine, *Controversy with Pelagius*

Human weakness cannot accomplish anything that has to do with salvation by itself alone, i.e., without the aid of God.

—John Cassian, *The Third Conference of Abbot Chaeremon*

For, if without Him we are able to do nothing actually, we are able neither to begin nor to perfect, —because to begin, it is said, "His mercy shall precede me!"; to finish, it is said, "His mercy shall follow me."

—Augustine, *Controversy with Pelagius*

In order to believe truly in the Son, we must believe that He is the Son.

—Clement of Alexandria, *The Stromata*

God is good, God is just. He is able to deliver some men without good merits, because He is good. He is able to condemn no man without evil desserts, because He is just.

—Augustine, *Against Julian*

Full salvation

If anyone has hoped in Christ as a Man lacking a mind, he is truly mindless and is quite unworthy of being saved. That which was not assumed has not been healed; but that which is united to God, the same is saved. If only half of Adam fell, then what is assumed and saved may also be only half; but if the whole of Adam fell, it must be united as a whole to Him that is born, in order to be wholly saved.

—Gregory of Nazianzus, *Letter to Cledonius the Priest, Against Apollinaris*

Urgent

God has promised forgiveness to your repentance; but He has not promised tomorrow to your procrastination.

—Augustine

God says "today"; the devil says "tomorrow".

—Basil the Great

N.B.

The salvation in which we believe is proved not from clever reasoning, but from the Holy Scriptures.

—Cyril of Jerusalem, *Catechetical Lectures*

Satan

(See also: Devil)

Deceiver deceived

For since that Deceiver thought that he was unconquerable in his malice, after he had cheated us with the hope of becoming gods, he was himself cheated by God's assumption of our nature; so that in attacking Adam as he thought, he should really meet with God. . . .

—Gregory of Nazianzus, *Oration on the Holy Lights*

The devil cannot conquer or subdue any but those who are in league with sin; and therefore he is conquered in the name of Him Who assumed humanity and that without sin. . . .

—Augustine, *The City of God*

Limited power

(Man is) not the sole author of . . . evil, but there is also another most wicked prompter, the devil. He indeed suggests, but does not get the mastery by force over those who do not consent.

—Cyril of Jerusalem, *Catechetical Lectures*

He is . . . most savage when he fully feels that a man is freed *from* his *clutches;* he then flames fiercest while he is fast becoming extinguished.

—Tertullian, *On Repentance*

The devil . . . has a will that cannot repent.

—Cyril of Jerusalem, *Catechetical Lectures*

⇹ Giving Satan too much credit

The more simple among believers in the Lord Christ are of opinion . . . if, for example there were no devil, no single human being would go astray. We, however . . . do not hold this opinion, taking into account those (sins) which manifestly originate as a necessary consequence of our bodily constitution.

—Origen, *De Principiis*

In the matter of eating and drinking it was possible for us to go wrong, even without any incitement from the devil, if we should happen to be either less temperate or less careful (than we ought); and we are to suppose, then, in our appetite for sexual intercouse, or in the restraint of our natural desires, our condition is not something similar?

—Origen *De Principiis*

Let us not wait for the repentance of the devil; for this is a vain anticipation and one that will drag us into the deep of hell.

—Jerome, *Letter to Pammachius and Oceanus*

⇹ Dialogue between Satan and Death

I heard Death and Satan, as they disputed, which was the more powerful, among men. . . . Death showed his power, that he conquers all; Satan showed his guile, that he makes all sin.

Death: To thee, O Evil One, none hearkens save he that wills; to me he that wills and he that wills not, even to me they come.

Satan: Thine, O Death, is but the force of tyranny; mine are snares and nets of subtlety.

Death: Hear, O Evil One, that who so is subtle breaks off thy yoke: but none is there that is able to escape my yoke.

Satan: Thou, Death, on him that is sick provest thy might: but I over them that are whole, am exceeding powerful.

Death: The Evil One prevails not over all those that revile him: but for me he that has cursed me and he that curses me, come into my hands.

Satan: Thou, Death, from God has gotten thy might: I alone by none am I helped, when I lead men to sin. . . .

Death: On Death there are many that call, as on a kind Power: on thee, O Evil One, none has called or calls. . . .

Satan: For thee, O Death, they hate thy name, and also thy work: my name they hate but my delights they greatly love.

Death: To bitterness of teeth is turned, this thy sweetness: penitence of soul cleaves ever unto thy lusts.

Satan: Sheol is hated because in her is no repentance: a pit that swallows and closes on all movements.

Death: Sheol is a gulf wherein whoso falls shall rise again: sin is hated because it cuts off the hope of man.

Satan: Though I dislike penitents, I give place for repentance: thou cuttest off hope from the sinner who dies in his sin.

Death: It was of thee that at first his hope was cut off: for he whom thou hast not caused to sin dies happily.

Blessed is He who raised against each other those cursed servants: that we might see them as they have seen us and mocked at us. This that we have seen of them is a pledge, my brethren: of what we shall see of them hereafter when we rise again.

—Ephraim the Syrian, *Nisibene Hymns*

Another dialogue between Satan and Death

Come, let us hear how they contend for victory: the guilty ones who never have conquered, nor will conquer. Death said unto the Evil One, in the end the victory is mine: for Death is master of the close. . . .

Satan: This dying of the body, is sleep for a time: think not, O Death, that thou are Death, who art as a shadow.

Death: Thee, O Evil One, the just have conquered, yea will conquer: but these that have conquered thee, lo! I conquer.

Satan: Even this that thou bringest to death the just, is not of thyself: because of Adam whom I conquered, they drink this cup.

Death: Lo! Sheol is full of the men of Sodom, and the Assyrians: and the giants who were in the flood, who is like me?

Satan: These, O Death, all of them, by me were slain: I am he that caused them to sin, so that they perished.

Death: Joseph who conquered thee I conquered, O Satan: in the chamber he conquered thee but I conquered, and cast him into the tomb.

Satan: Moses who conquered thee, O Death, by sprinkling of blood: he conquered thee in Egypt, but at the rock, who conquered him?

Death: Elijah who feared thee not, O Satan: fled before Jezebel's face, because he feared me.

Satan: Aaron who withstood thee, O Death, with smoke of incense: to him I gave earrings of gold: and he fashioned a calf.

Death: Thou wentest down to contend with Job, and he conquered thee and came up: but I, after he had conquered thee, then conquered him.

Satan: David who by his sackcloth stayed that pestilence: him on the house-top I conquered, who had conquered Goliath.

Death: Jehu who destroyed the house of Baal, the temple of the Evil One: was unable to destroy Sheol, the stronghold of my realm.

Satan: Solomon who snatched from thy mouth, a child by his judgment: him in his old age I made a builder of idol-altars.

Death: Samuel who in respect of gold scorned thee, O Satan: him I conquered, the conqueror, who conquered bribes.

Satan: Samson who in respect of the lion's whelp, scorned thee, O Death: through Delilah, frail vessel, I yoked him to the mill.

Death: Josiah from his childhood despised thee, Evil One: but me not even in his old age, could he withstand.

Satan: Hezekiah withstood thee, Death, when he overcame the bound of life: I misled him and he neglected the miracle, and showed his treasures.

Death: John who conquered thee, Evil One, and absolved and baptized: I extinguished that torch, which had disclosed thee.

Satan: Simon overcame thee, when he brought to life that blessed woman: in a woman he overcame thee and by a woman I overcame him and made him deny. . . . Apostles and prophets with one voice, curse thee, O Death: "Where is the victory of Death, and the sting of Sheol?"

—Ephraim the Syrian, *Nisibene Hymns*

School of Christ

(See also: Instruction)

God has always something to teach, and man always something to learn from Him.

—Irenaeus, *Against Heresies*

And if, too, the end of the wise man is contemplation, that of those who are still philosophers aim at it, but never attains it, unless by the process of learning it receives the prophetic utterance which has been made known. . . .

—Clement of Alexandria, *The Stromata*

For by teaching, one learns more.

—Clement of Alexandria, *The Stromata*

It is a fine thing to teach, if the speaker practise.

—Ignatius, *Letter to the Ephesians*

She must not therefore learn as a child what afterwards she will have to unlearn.

—Jerome, *Letter to Laeta*

Nor could there be any better ornaments for the ears than true instruction.

—Clement of Alexandria, *The Paedagogus*

. . . two reasons the teaching of spiritual things is ineffectual. For either the teacher is commending what he has no experience of, and is trying with empty-sounding words to instruct his hearer, or else the hearer is a bad man and full of faults and cannot receive in his hard heart the holy and saving doctrine of the spiritual man.

—John Cassian, *The First Conference of Abbot Nesteros*

Still learning

For even I, though I am bound, and am able to understand heavenly things, the angelic orders, and the different sorts of angels and hosts, the distinction between powers and dominions, and the diversities between thrones and authorities, the mightiness of the Aeons, and preeminence of the cherubim and seraphim, the sublimity of the spirit, the Kingdom of the Lord, and above all the incomparable majesty of Almighty God—though I am acquainted with these things, yet am I not therefore by any means perfect; nor am I such a disciple as Paul or Peter. For many things are yet wanting to me, that I may not fall short of God.

—Ignatius, *Epistle to the Trallians*

You have missed the profit of your calamity.

—Augustine, *The City of God*

Dangers of too rapid promotion

One who was yesterday a catechumen is today a bishop; one who was yesterday in the amphitheater is today in the church; one who spent the evening in the circus stands in the morning at the altar.

—Jerome, *Letter to Oceanus*

A wise curriculum

Let her begin by learning the psalter, and then let her gather rules of life out of the proverbs of Solomon. From the preacher let her gain the habit of despising the world and its vanities. Let her follow the example set in Job of virtue and of patience. Then let her pass on to the gospels never to be laid aside when once thay have been taken in hand. Let her also drink in with a willing heart the Acts of the Apostles and the Epistles. As soon as she has enriched the storehouse of her mind with these treasures, let her commit to memory the prophets, the heptateuch, the books of Kings and of Chronicles, the rolls also of Ezra and Esther. When she has done all these she may safely read the Song of Songs but not before.

—Jerome, *Letter to Laeta*

N.B.

No one blushes at his own improvement.

—Tertullian, *On Modesty*

Second Birth

(See also: Salvation)

Every soul is considered as having been born in Adam until it has been reborn in Christ. Moreover, it is unclean until it has been regenerated.

—Tertullian

It is not the equity of nature, but the ambition of evil desire, which has given rise to worldly nobility. Unquestionably, we are all rendered equal by the grace of the divine bath (baptism), and there can be no difference among those, whom the second birth has generated, by means of which alike the rich man and the poor man . . . is rendered a son of God.

—Sulpitius Severus, *Letter to Claudia*

He that was to inaugurate a new kind of birth must Himself be born in a new way. . . .

—Tertullian, *The Flesh of Christ*

Second Coming

(See also: Eschatology; Prophecy)

The two comings

Oh, foolish people! They do not understand what has been proved again and again, that two manifestations of His arrival are prophesied: in the one He suffers, is robbed of glory and honour, and is crucified as was prophesied; in the other He will appear in glory from Heaven.

—Justin, *Dialogue with Trypho the Jew*

For all things, for the most part, are twofold in our Lord Jesus Christ: a twofold generation; one, of God, before the ages; and one, of a Virgin, at the close of the ages: His coming twofold; one, the unobserved, like rain on a fleece; and a second His open coming, which is to be. In His former advent, He was wrapped in swaddling clothes in the manger; in His second, He covereth Himself with light as with a garment. In His first coming, He endured the Cross, despising shame; in His second, He comes attended by a host of angels, receiving glory.

—Cyril of Jerusalem, *Lecture*

When?

That day lies hid that every day we be on the watch.

—Augustine

It is not expedient for the apostles to know, so that always uncertain of the coming of the Judge, they may live daily as if they were to be judged perhaps on that very day.

—Jerome, *Commentaries on the Gospel of Matthew*

He who loves the coming of the Lord is not he who affirms it is far off, nor is it he who says it is near. It is he who, whether it be far or near, awaits it with sincere faith, steadfast hope and fervent love.

—Augustine

We pray for the postponement of the end.

—Tertullian, *Apology*

"When you do not expect it, He will come," because He wants them to be anxiously waiting, and constantly engaged in virtuous practice. What He means is something like this: "If the generality of men knew when they were to die, they would strive earnestly (only) at that hour."

—John Chrysostom, *Homilies on the Gospel of Matthew*

How?

But if they say that He will come at the end of the world without a body, how shall those "see Him that pierced Him"?

—Ignatius, *Epistle to the Smyrnaeans*

In the first advent God veiled His divinity to prove the faithful; in the second advent He will manifest His glory to reward their faith.

—John Chrysostom

This Jesus Christ who is gone up shall come again, not from earth but from heaven: and I say, "not from earth," because there are many antichrists to come at this time from earth.

—Cyril of Jerusalem, *Catechetical Lectures*

N.B.

Consider the times: look for Him who is above time.

—Ignatius, *Epistle to the Ephesians*

With reason, then, does Christ's disciple ask food for himself for the day, since he is prohibited from thinking of the morrow; because it becomes a contradiction and a repugnant thing for us to seek to live long in this world, since we ask that the Kingdom of God should come quickly.

—Cyprian, *Treatise on the Lord's Prayer*

Selfishness

(See also: Pride)

By selfishness, I mean a passion whose object is the body.

—Maximus, *The Centuries on Charity*

Though I have left the city's haunts, as the source of innumerable ills, yet I have not yet learned to leave myself.

—Basil, *Letter to Gregory of Nazianzus*

Of myself I made a desert land.

—Augustine, *Confessions*

N.B.

Let virtue consume what was provided for self-indulgence.

—Jerome, *Letter to Furia*

Sex

(See also: Love; Lust)

Boundaries

God has fixed the bounds of lawful desire not only within the walls of one house but also within the narrow limits of one bed.

—Lactantius Firmianus, *The Divine Institutes*

What is unlawful in church cannot be lawful at home.

—Jerome, *Letter to Pammachius*

This passion and this impulse is found in man to be more vehement and more intense than in any other animal; either because God wished that mankind should surpass all other creatures in number, or else, having given virtue to man alone, He meant him in checking his pleasures to win the praise and glory of self-restraint.

—Lactantius Firmianus, *The Divine Institutes*

They must be frankly told either to marry if they cannot contain, or to contain if they will not marry.

—Jerome, *Letter to Demetrias*

⇹ The higher law

Even if the body be free from stain, no credit for modesty can be given, if the heart is impure.

—Lactantius Firmianus, *The Divine Institutes*

We are so far from practising promiscuous intercourse that we are not even allowed a lustful glance. What could justify any doubt as to the purity of the life led by those who are not allowed to use their eyes for any other purpose than that for which God created them, namely to look in the light, for whom even a lustful glance is called adultery! For them the coming judgment applies even to thoughts!

—Athenagoras, *A Plea Regarding Christians*

⇹ Equality of the sexes

Their laws are unequal and irregular. Why did they restrain the woman but indulge the man? A woman who practices evil against her husband's bed is guilty of adultery, and for this the penalties of the law are very severe; but a husband committing fornication against his wife, has he no account to give? I do not accept this legislation nor do I approve this custom. . . . This is not how God acts. He says, "Honor thy father and thy mother."

—Gregory of Nazianzus, *On the Words of the Gospel in Matthew*

⇹ Sex in the afterlife?

He foretold that, in the future world, sexual intercourse should be done away with (Luke 20:34–35).

—Justin, *On the Resurrection*

"For in the resurrection they neither marry nor are given in marriage but are as the angels." When it is said that they neither marry nor are given in marriage, the distinction of sex is shewn to persist.

—Jerome, *Letter to Eustochium*

N.B.

It is no credit therefore not to do that which you cannot do.

—Lactantius Firmianus, *The Divine Institutes*

Silence

A properly kept silence is a beautiful thing; it is nothing less than the father of very wise thoughts.

—Diodicus, *One Hundred Chapters on Spiritual Perfection*

Christ saved men not with thunder and lighting but as a wailing babe in the manger and as a silent sufferer upon the cross.

—Jerome, *Letter to Theophilus, Bishop of Alexandria*

The sounds of our voice, likewise, should be subdued; else, if we are to be heard for our noise, how large windpipes should we need! But God is the hearer not of the *voice*, but of the *heart*.

—Tertullian, *On Prayer*

Her speech is silent and her silence is speech.

—Jerome, *Letter to Marcella*

N.B.

That Thou mayest be understood, we must be silent.

—Arnobius, *Against the Heathen*

⇜ Sin ⇝

(See also: Evil; Vice)

⇜ Sin?

The serpent's deadly venom.

—Ausonius, *The Daily Routine*

Evil . . . nothing else than corruption.

—Augustine, *The Nature of the Good*

Whatever is done through error of reason is transgression, and is rightly called sin. Since, then, the first man sinned and disobeyed God, it is said, "And man became like to the beasts": being rightly regarded as irrational, he is likened to the beasts.

—Clement of Alexandria, *The Instructor*

I preach and think that it is more bitter to sin against Christ than to suffer the torments of hell.

—John Chrysostom

Two kinds of blindness easily combine; those who fail to see what really is, fancy that they see what is not. . . .

—Tertullian, *The Christian Defence*

Every lesser good has an essential element of sin.

—Augustine

With us, it is a sin even to consider a crime. You fear witnesses. We fear even our own conscience.

—Minucius Felix, *Octavius*

This is the crowning guilt of men, that they do not want to know Him of whom they cannot be ignorant.

—Tertullian, *Apology*

What can sin be? . . . It is not an enemy, O man, that assails thee from without, but an evil shoot growing up out of thyself.

—Cyril of Jerusalem, *Catechetical Lecture*

Security in sin is likewise an appetite for it.

—Tertullian, *On Modesty*

Sin then is . . . a fearful evil, but not incurable.

—Cyril of Jerusalem, *Catechetical Lectures*

Degrees of sin?

Although they commit lesser evils because they are capable only of lesser evils, they are, however, not less evil because they would not want to be less if they could. . . .

—Salvian, *The Governance of God*

We acknowledge that there are certain sins in brethren which are more heinous than the persecution of enemies.

—Augustine, *Our Lord's Sermon on the Mount*

An adulteress against Christ is more guilty than one against her husband.

—Sulpitius Severus, *Letter to Claudia*

Do not make light even of those sins called lesser. If you make light of them when you weigh them, be terrified when you count them.

—Augustine, *Homilies on the Epistle of John*

First of all it must be understood that this distinction has no basis in the New Testament. A single declaration is made against all sins, when the Lord says, "He that sins is the slave of sin." . . . If, however, we can safely speak of small and great sin, it is incontrovertibly evident to everyone that a great sin is one that holds anyone in its power, whereas a small sin is one which does not get the upper hand. . . .

—Basil the Great, *Rules Briefly Treated*

Is the sinless life possible?

A man, helped by God, can, if he will, be without sin. But ask me the second question, whether or not there really is such a sinless man, and I will say that I believe there is not.

—Augustine, *Forgiveness of Sins*

I said that it was my wish not to sin, and you, no doubt also have the same desire. Therefore, why is it neither of us can do what each of us wants to do?

—Jerome, *Dialogue Against the Pelagians*

No conception is without iniquity, since there are no parents who have not fallen.

—Ambrose of Milan, *Explanation of David the Prophet*

For no one is ever driven to sin by being provoked through another's fault unless he has the fuel of evil stored up in his own heart.

—John Cassian, *The Institutes of John Cassian*

At the fall, man's natural gifts were corrupted through sin, while his supernatural gifts were entirely lost.

—Augustine

Of the flesh and of the spirit

Every sin is a matter either of *act* or else of *thought*: so that what is in *deed* is "corporeal" because a *deed*, like a body, is capable of being *seen* and *touched*; what is in the *mind* is "spiritual," because *spirit* is neither *seen* nor *handled*: by which consideration is shown that sins not of *deed* only, but of *will* too, are to be shunned, and by repentance purged. For if human finitude judges only sins of deed, because it is not equal to (piercing) the lurking-places of the *will*, let us not on that account make light of crimes of the will in God's sight. God is all-sufficient.

—Tertullian, *On Repentance*

Sins of the saints

For it is an impossibility for any one of the saints not to fall into those trivial faults which are committed by the word, and thought, and ignorance, and forgetfulness, and necessity, and will, and surprise: which though quite different from that sin which is said to be unto death, still cannot be free from fault and blame.

—John Cassian, *The First Conference of Abbot Chaeremon*

It is this difference in their sins which separate Judas the betrayer from Peter the denier: not that a penitent is not to be pardoned, for we must not come into collision with that declaration of our Lord . . . but that the ruin connected with that sin is so great, that he cannot endure the humiliation of asking for it, even if he should be compelled by a bad conscience both to acknowledge and divulge his sin. For when Judas had said, "I have sinned, in that I have betrayed the innocent blood," yet it was easier for him in despair to run and hang himself, than in humility to ask for pardon.

—Augustine, *Our Lord's Sermon on the Mount*

Original sin

They . . . who beget, even if they themselves are already regenerate, beget not as children of God, but as still being children of the world.

—Augustine, *Marriage and Concupiscence*

Their intercourse took place after the transgression; until then they had behaved in Paradise like angels, not burning with desire, nor beset by other passions, not subject to the necessities of nature, but, created entirely incorruptible and immortal, there they had no need even for the protective covering of garments.

—John Chrysostom, *Homilies on Genesis*

Before we are born we are infected with the contagion, and before we see the light of day we experience the injury of our origin.

—Ambrose of Milan, *Explanation of David the Prophet*

How is original sin transferred?

By the law of semination and germination. . . .

—Augustine, *Against Julian's Second Reply*

The ultimate target

For no one does decline him that is visible, but does (in reality) seek to mock Him that is invisible, who, however, cannot be mocked by any one. . . . For God says to Samuel, "They have not mocked thee, but Me." And Moses declares, "For their murmuring is not against us, but against the Lord God."

—Ignatius, *Epistle to the Magnesians*

This fear in me is . . . of long standing, that I should win honour from men at the price of sinning against God.

—Synesius, *To his brother*

Think, brother, what sin it must be which has God for its opponent.

—Jerome, *Letter to Anthony Monk*

For sinning we have no help from God.

—Augustine, *Forgiveness of Sins*

N.B.

Every sin is dischargeable either by pardon or else by penalty: by pardon as the result of chastisement, by penalty as the result of condemnation.

—Tertullian, *On Modesty*

Social Graces

That clergyman soon becomes an object of contempt who being often asked out to dinner never refuses to go.

—Jerome, *Letter to Nepotian*

Answer not a word before you hear.

—Clement of Alexandria, *The Instructor*

Let your conversation be marked with such confidence that the entry of a third person shall neither startle you nor make you blush.

—Jerome, *Letter to Furia*

For we are not to copy oxen and asses, whose manger and dunghill are together. For many wipe their noses and spit even whilst supping.

—Clement of Alexandria, *The Instructor*

Do not, I pray, put off modesty at the same time that you put off your clothes.

—Clement of Alexandria, *The Instructor*

Soul

So great is the dignity of souls that each one has from the beginning of his birth an angel delegated to guard him.

—Jerome, *Commentaries on the Gospel of Matthew*

There are many people who exert greater care for their bodies than they do for their soul. But they should devote a greater solicitude for their souls, where the image of God is. When the flesh, which they love so much, begins to be devoured by worms in the grave, the soul is presented to God by the angels in heaven.

—Caesar of Arles, *Sermons*

In the soul of man there is reason, which is not present in the beast. Therefore, just as the soul is superior to the body, so too in the soul itself reason is superior.

—Augustine, *Against Faustus the Manichean*

There are three states of the soul—ignorance, opinion, knowledge—those who are in ignorance are the Gentiles, those in knowledge, the true Church, and those in opinion, the Heretics.

—Clement of Alexandria, *The Stromata*

We are convinced that there exist two men in each one of us. The one is confessedly a hidden thing, while the other stands apparent; one is corporeal, the other spiritual although the generation of both may be compared to that of twins. For both are revealed to the world as but one, for the soul was not anterior to the body in its essence; nor, in regard to its formation, did the body precede the soul: but both these were produced at one time; and their nourishment consists in purity and sweetness.

—Irenaeus, *Fragments from Lost Writings*

N.B.

God desires a beauty not of the body, but of the soul.

—Sulpitius Severus, *Letter to Claudia*

The State

The two realms

Give to Caesar what is Caesar's—his image on the coin; give God what is God's—His image in man, yourself.

—Tertullian

The tribute that belongs to Caesar is not to be denied. The Church, however, is God's, and it must not be pledged to Caesar.

—Ambrose of Milan, *Sermon Against Auxentius*

From the king's office, laws, the priest's office, propitiations. That both should be mild is hateful; that both should be strong is grievous. Let one be strong and one be tender; in prudence and in discretion, let fear with mercy be mingled. . . . Blessed be He Who has mingled our helps!

—Ephraim the Syrian, *Nisibene Hymns*

Let the priests pray for the kings, that they may be a wall to mankind! From beside the kings be victory; and from beside the priests faith! May victory save our bodies, and faith our souls! May kings put an end to war; priests put an end to strife!

—Ephriam the Syrian, *Nisibene Hymns*

The Church is not in the Empire, but the Emperor is in the Church.

—Ambrose of Milan

Give obedience

Consider that every command of the emperor which does not offend God has proceeded from God Himself.

—Theonas of Alexandria, *Epistle to Lucianus*

Christians are benefactors of their country more than others. For they train up citizens, and inculcate piety to the Supreme Being; and they promote those whose lives in the smallest cities have been good and worthy, to a divine and heavenly city.

—Origen, *Against Celsus*

If the providence of God does not govern human affairs there is no point in troubling oneself about religion.

—Augustine, *The Advantage of Believing*

As we by our prayers vanquish all demons who stir up war, and lead to the violation of oaths, and disturb the peace, we in this way are much more helpful to the kings than those who go into the field to fight for them.

—Origen, *Against Celsus*

Misuse of power

In their (Christians) case the practice of torture was reversed; it was employed not to elicit the truth, but to compel people to lie.

—Minucius Felix, *Octavius*

Advice to rulers

Let him be a patient ruler; let him know when he may relax the reins; let him terrify at first, and then anoint with honey; and let him first observe to do himself what he says.

—Commodianus, *Instructions*

N.B.

Caesar is more ours than yours, for our God appointed him.

—Tertullian

Suffering

The glory of wounds

In the servant of God, the glory of the wounds made the victory; the memory of the scars preserves that glory.

—Cyprian, *Epistles*

It is not the suffering, but the cause, that makes men martyrs.

—Augustine, *Psalms*

He who fears to suffer cannot be His who suffered.

—Tertullian, *De Fuga in Persecutione*

Voluntary pain is a higher thing than involuntary comfort.

—Gregory of Nazianzus, *To Basil*

A reason why good people suffer

This seems to me to be one principal reason why the good are chastised along with the wicked . . . not because they have spent an equally corrupt life, but because the good as well as the wicked, though not equally with them, love this present life; while they ought to hold it cheap, that the wicked, being admonished and reformed by their example, might lay hold of life eternal. And if they will not be the companions of the good in seeking life everlasting, they should be loved as enemies.

—Augustine, *The City of God*

N.B.

I had . . . the luxury of suffering hardship with you.

—Gregory of Nazianzus, *To Basil*

Sunday

The Day of the Sun is the day on which we all gather in a common meeting, because it is the first day, the day on which God, changing darkness and matter, created the world; and it is the day on which Jesus Christ our Saviour rose from the dead.

—Justin Martyr, *First Apology*

If circumcision was not necessary before Abraham, nor before Moses, the sabbath observance and festivals and sacrifices, then, similarly, they are not necessary now. . . .

—Justin Martyr, *Dialogue with Trypho the Jew*

The fathers of old received . . . the circumcision of the flesh on the eighth day after birth . . . (Our Lord) put a seal on the Sunday by His resurrection. The Sunday is the third day after His passion, but the octave day as well, indeed the first octave, if we count the days that follow on the Saturday.

—Augustine, *The Lord's Prayer Explained*

Temptation

(See also: Trials)

When evil desire finds you armed with the fear of God and determined to resist, it will flee far away from you.

—Hermas, *The Shepherd*

It is not those that abstain from wickedness from compulsion, but those that abstain from choice, that God crowns.

—Clement of Alexandria, *Maximus, Sermon 55*

A true eunuch is not one who is unable, but one who is unwilling, to indulge in pleasure.

—Clement of Alexandria, *The Instructor*

What difference is there between being tempted, and falling or entering into temptation? Well, if one is overcome of evil . . . that man has entered into temptation, and is in it, and is brought under it like one that is led captive. But if one withstands and endures, that man is indeed tempted; but he has not entered into temptation or fallen into it.

—Dionysius the Great, *Exegetical Fragments*

Which has more truly apostatized—he who has lost Christ amid agonies, or amid delights?

—Tertullian, *On Modesty*

⇹ Pseudo-strategies

He who is sometimes grieving, and is sometimes enjoying himself and laughing, is like a man pelting the dog of voluptuousness with bread, who chases it in appearance, but in fact invites it to remain near him.

—Clement of Alexandria, *Sermon 17 from Antonius Melissa*

⇹ Confessions of the Tempter

I (Satan) tempted Him . . . with pleasant bread, but He desired it not. To my grief I strove to learn a psalm, that by His psalm I might take Him as a prey: I paused and learned it a second time, but He made my second trial to be vain. I brought Him up to a mountain and showed Him all possessions; I gave them to Him and He was not moved. Better was it for me in the days of Adam, who gave me no great trouble in teaching him.

—Ephraim the Syrian, *Nisibene Hymns*

The lust of the body, is in all bodies; for even while they sleep, it wakes in them. Him, who in his waking hours keeps himself pure, by means of a dream, I (Satan) disturb. The dregs of the body are stirred in him, by a shaking movement in secret inwardly. The sleeping and the waking besides, I trouble alike. This is He (Christ) Who alone keeps Himself pure, Whom not even in a dream can I disturb, Who even in His sleep is pure and holy.

—Ephraim the Syrian, *Nisibene Hymns*

⇹ How could Christ be tempted?

. . . through suggestion; but the pleasure of sin did not get its teeth into His mind; and therefore every diabolic temptation was from without, not from within.

—Gregory the Great, *Homilies on the Gospels*

N.B.

To err is human, but to lay snares is diabolical.

—Jerome, *The Apology Against the Books of Rufinus*

Thankfulness

Therefore we ought to give most fervent thanks to the Lord, for making known to us the past, for giving us light about the present, and for not leaving us without discernment of the future.

—Barnabas, *A Letter*

The Christian, even when condemned to die, gives thanks.

—Tertullian

Time

What, then, is time? If no one asked me, I know; but, if I want to explain it to a questioner, I do not know.

—Augustine, *Confessions*

I say with confidence that I know that, if nothing passed away, there would be no past time; if nothing were coming, there would be no future time; and if nothing were existing, there would be no present time.

—Augustine, *Confessions*

Tongue

"Helps" to curb

Let your conversation always be temperate and modest, and

seasoned with religion as with salt.

—Theonas of Alexandria, *Epistle to Lucianus*

The tongue is to be moderately bridled, not to be bound immoderately.

—Gregory the Great, *Pastoral Care*

Make it your object, therefore, to keep your tongue chaste as well as your eyes.

—Jerome, *Letter to Nepotian*

Blessed, assuredly, are the lips, which never utter what they would wish to recall.

—Sulpitius Severus, *Letter to Claudia*

The man who cannot restrain his tongue is most like an open city . . . it is much the easier to overcome, because it fights against itself with loquacity, helping the adversary.

—Gregory the Great, *Pastoral Care*

Excessive treatment

If often happens . . . when they excessively restrain their tongues, they are much more severely afflicted in their hearts than the loquacious, since their thoughts boil in their hearts.

—Gregory the Great, *Pastoral Care*

The hidden is more painful than the open wound, for when the matter which collects in it is allowed to escape, the wound is opened and the pain relieved.

—Gregory the Great, *Pastoral Care*

N.B.

And it is with triflers as with old shoes: all the rest is worn away by evil; the tongue only is left for destruction.

—Clement of Alexandria, *The Instructor*

Tradition

Church traditions—especially when they do not run counter to faith—are to be observed in the form in which previous generations have handed them down; and the use of one church is not to be annulled because it is contrary to that of another.

—Jerome, *Letter to Lucinius*

Trials

(See also: Temptation)

When a trial comes upon you suddenly, do not react against him through whom it comes, but find out its object, and then you will find a way of profiting from it. From wherever it may have come, you would still have to empty the bitter cup of God's decrees!

—Maximus, *The Centuries on Charity*

The prudent man, seeing recovery in the divine decrees, receives with gratitude the misfortunes which they bring; they have, he tells himself, no other cause than his own sins.

—Maximus, *The Centuries on Charity*

Trinity

Attempts at definition

There is a perfect Trinity, in glory and eternity and sovereignity, neither divided nor estranged. Wherefore there is nothing either created or in servitude in the Trinity; nor anything superinduced, as if at some former period it was nonexistent, and at some later period it was introduced. And this neither was the Son ever wanting to the Father nor the Spirit to the Son; but without variation and without change, the same Trinity *abideth* ever.

—Gregory of Nyssa, quoted by Gregory of Neocaesarea in *Panegyric to Origen*

It is consistent in Itself, indivisible in nature, and Its activity is one.

—Athanasius, *Four Letters to Serapion*

For to us there is but One God, the Father, of Whom are all things; and one Lord Jesus Christ, by Whom are all things; and one Holy Ghost, in Whom are all things.

—Gregory of Nazianzus, *Fifth Theological Oration*

This grace on Thy redeemed confer, Father, coequal Son, and Holy Ghost, the Comforter, Eternal, three in one.

—Ambrose, *The Hymns of the Little Hours*

In the Father there is unity, in the Son equality, and in the Holy Spirit the harmony of unity and equality; and these three are all one because of the Father, all equal because of the Son, all connected because of the Holy Spirit.

—Augustine, *Christian Instruction*

When the Lord gave us the formula of the Father, the Son, and the Holy Spirit, He did not connect the gift with number. . . . Let the Unapproachable be altogether above and beyond number, in the same way that the ancient reverence of the Hebrews wrote the unutterable name of God in characters reserved, attempting thereby to proclaim its infinite excellence. Count if you must; but you must not by your counting do damage to the faith.

—Basil the Great, *The Holy Spirit*

Common to Father and Son and Holy Spirit is their having no coming into being, and their divinity. Common to Son and Holy Spirit is their coming from the Father. Proper to the Father alone is His unbegottenness; to the Son alone, His begottenness; to the Spirit alone, His being sent forth.

—Gregory of Nazianzus, *In Praise of Hero the Philosopher*

We accept that there is a distinction and not a confusion of Father and of Son and of Holy Spirit; a distinction, but not a separation; a distinction but not a plurality.

—Ambrose of Milan, *The Faith*

Attempts at description

Even when a ray is shot forth from the sun it is a part of the whole; but the sun will be in the ray because it is a ray of the sun, not separated from its substance but extended therefrom, as light is enkindled from light. . . . So also, that which proceeds from God is God and Son of God, and both are one. Likewise, as He is Spirit from Spirit, and God from God, He is made a second by count and in numerical sequence, but not in actual condition; for He comes forth from the source but does not separate therefrom.

—Tertullian, *Apology*

The three days before the luminaries were created are types of the Trinity: God, His Word, and His Wisdom.

—Theophilus of Antioch, *To Autolycus*

We think of those three elements in the mind of man: memory, intelligence, and will. . . .

—Augustine, *Against a Discourse of the Arians*

For the One was from the beginning, then the Three were so too. . . . For what profit is there in an imperfect Godhead?

—Gregory of Nazianzus, *On the Holy Spirit*

If we were to speak of many gods it would be necessary to recognize a difference among the many. But if there is no difference among them, there is but one and not many.

—John Damascene, *The Source of Knowledge*

To those who accuse us of a doctrine of three Gods, let it be stated that we confess one God, not in number but in nature.

—Evagrius of Pontus, *Dogmatic Letter on the Most Blessed Trinity*

He is not other by division but by distinction.

—Tertullian, *Against Praxeas*

Without variation and without change, the same Trinity forever.

—Gregory, the miracle worker, *The Creed*

The Godhead is common; the fatherhood particular. We must therefore combine the two and say, "I believe in God the Father." The like course must be pursued in the confession of the Son; we must combine the particular with the common and say, "I believe in God the Son," so in the case of the Holy Ghost we must make our utterance conform to the appellation and say, "in God the Holy Ghost."

—Basil of Caesarea, *Epistle 236*

Father and Son

Since, therefore, the Father is eternal, the Son . . . is eternal. If there is a parent, there is also a child.

—Dionysius the Great, *Refutation and Defense*

By confessing the Father, it confesses the Son. Believing in the Father, it believes also in the Son, because the name *father* has in itself the name *son*. For there is no father except through a son . . . there is no son except through a father.

—Hilary of Poitiers, *The Trinity*

The Father is greater than the Son: but this is said in respect to generation—as a father is to a son—and not of classification.

—Hilary of Poitiers, *Commentaries on the Psalms*

I would not hesitate to call the Son a stem from the root and a river from the fountain and a ray from the sun; because every source is a parent, and everything that issues from the source is an offspring. . . . The stem is not separated from the root nor the river from the fountain, nor the ray from the sun. Neither, then, is the Word separated from God.

—Tertullian, *Against Praxeas*

That which is in the Father is in the Son also; that which is in the Unbegotten is in the Only-begotten also; One from the Other, and both are One.

—Hilary of Poitiers, *The Trinity*

What is the Son of Him that is the Father? Another the same.

—Gregory of Elvira, *The Orthodox Faith*

He that is the Son of God by being generated and who is coeternal always with the Father—the same One begins to be Son of Man from the Virgin. And so too humanity is added to the Son's divinity; and yet, no quaternity of Persons results, but the Trinity remains.

—Augustine, *Sermons*

"The Father and I, we are one." He teaches us that *one* refers to Their nature, and *we are* to Their persons.

—Fulgence of Ruspe, *The Trinity*

The Trinity remains a Trinity even after the Incarnation of the Word.

—John Damascene, *The Source of Knowledge*

Would you have considered the One who reconciled us to His Father to be a stranger to that Father?

—Athanasius, *Resurrection Letter VIII*

Son and Holy Spirit

The Lord Jesus Himself has not only, as God, given the Holy Spirit, but also, as Man, He has received Him.

—Augustine, *The Trinity*

Never in the Scriptures is the Spirit called Son, lest He might be reckoned as a brother. Nor is He called son of the Son, lest the Father might be termed a grandfather.

—Athanasius, *Discourse Against the Arians*

Functions of the Trinity

And ye are prepared for the building of God the Father, and ye are raised up on high by the instrument of Jesus Christ, which is the cross; and ye are drawn by the rope, which is the Holy Spirit; and your pulley is your faith, and your love is the way which leadeth up on high to God.

—Ignatius, *Second Letter to the Ephesians*

He is *over all* as Father, as beginning, as source; and *through all*, through the Word; and *in all*, in the Holy Spirit.

—Athanasius, *Four Letters to Serapion*

The Father and the Son and the Holy Spirit are one in all respects except those of being unbegotten, of begetting, and of proceeding.

—John Damascene, *The Source of Knowledge*

The path to the knowledge of God lies *from* one Spirit *through* one Son *to* one Father. . . .

—Basil the Great, *The Holy Spirit*

Great is the mystery

That God is without beginning and unbegotten and eternal, I know; but how, I do not know. For reasoning is unable to grasp how some essence can exist without having existence either from itself or from another. I know that the Son has been begotten, but the how of it I do not know. I know that the Spirit is from Him, but the how of His being from Him I do not know.

—John Chrysostom, *Homilies Against the Anomoians*

If asked to define the Trinity, we can only say that it is not this or that.

—Augustine

He fixed the names of His nature: Father, Son, and Holy Spirit. Whatever is sought over and above this is beyond the meaning of words, beyond the limits of perception, beyond the embrace of understanding.

—Hilary of Poitiers, *The Trinity*

N.B.

They must be shunned as evidently hostile to piety who overturn the order given us by the Lord and place the Son before the Father, and the Holy Spirit before the Son.

—Basil the Great, *Letters*

Truth

Greeks contradict, Samaritans disbelieve, heretics mutilate. Contradiction is manifold, but truth is uniform.

—Cyril of Jerusalem, *Catechetical Lectures*

Faith . . . is to believe what you do not see, truth is to see what you have believed.

—Augustine, *Homilies on John*

Truth always shines brighter when thoroughly ventilated. . . .

—John Cassian, *The Seven Books of John Cassian*

It would have been easier to doubt that I am alive than to be in doubt whether truth might not exist.

—Augustine, *Confessions*

For it is in our power, when we are examined, to deny that we are Christians; but we would not live by telling a lie.

—Justin, *The First Apology*

We are more inclined to put faith in those who confess to their own disadvantage than in those who deny for their own advantage.

—Tertullian

N.B.

Seek for yourself, O man—search for your true self. "He who seeks shall find himself in God."

—Augustine, *Confessions*

Unity

Blessings of unity

Your accord and harmonious love is a hymn to Jesus Christ.

—Ignatius, *Letter to the Ephesians*

For many specious wolves with baneful delights lead captive the runners in God's race; but, where ye are at one, they will find no place.

—Ignatius, *Letter to the Philadelphians*

Curse of disunity

Holy Scripture declares in the books of Kings; when ten tribes were divided from the tribe of Judah and Benjamin, and forsaking their king, appointed for themselves another one without . . . so great was the indignation of the Lord against those who had made the schism, that even when the man of God was sent to Jeroboam, to charge upon him his sins, and predict the future vengeance, he was forbidden to eat bread or to drink water with them.

—Cyprian, *Epistles*

The Blessed Apostle John distinguished no heresy or schism,

neither did he set down any as specially separated; but he called all who had gone out from the Church, and who acted in opposition to the Church, antichrist. . . .

—Cyprian, *Epistles*

God is one, and Christ is one, and His Church is one, and the faith is one, and people are joined into a substantial unity of body by the cement of concord. Unity cannot be severed; nor can one body be separated by a division of its structure, nor torn into pieces, with its entrails wrenched asunder by laceration. Whatever has proceeded from the womb cannot live and breathe in its detached condition, but loses the substance of health.

—Cyprian, *Treatises*

N.B.

Avoid the wolves who separate the sheep from the shepherd.

—Cyprian, *Epistles*

Vice

(See also: Evil, Sin)

No one administers drugs till he has rubbed the rim of the cup with honey; so the better to deceive us, vice puts on the appearance and the semblance of virtue.

—Jerome, *Letter to Laeta*

We make ourselves a ladder out of our vices if we trample the vices themselves underfoot.

—Augustine, *De Ascensione*

Evil . . . nothing else than corruption.

—Augustine, *The Nature of the Good*

Virgin Birth

(See also: Incarnation; Nativity)

If you seek out the reason for this it will no longer be marvelous. If you demand a comparable example it will no longer be unique.

—Augustine, *Letter to Volusian*

Through Eve yet virgin came death; through a virgin, or rather from a virgin, must Life appear.

—Cyril of Jerusalem

Immaculate and undefiled was His generation: for where the Holy Spirit breathes, there all pollution is taken away: undefiled from the Virgin was the incarnate generation of the Only-begotten.

—Cyril of Jerusalem, *Catechetical Lecture XII*

A challenge to doubters and deniers

But those of the circumcision meet thou with this question: Whether is harder, for an aged woman, barren and past age, to bear, or for a virgin in the prime of youth to conceive? Sarah was barren, and though it had ceased to be with her after the manner of women, yet, contrary to nature, she bore a child. If, then, it is against nature for a barren woman to conceive, and also for a virgin to conceive, therefore, reject both, or accept both.

—Cyril of Jerusalem, *Catechetical Lecture XII*

If Eve was then born out of a man's side without a mother, and is a child not to be born without a father, of a virgin's womb?

—Cyril of Jerusalem, *Catechetical Lecture XII*

Virginity

(See also: Chastity)

I call virginity fine corn, wedlock barley, and fornication cow-dung.

—Jerome, *Letter to Pammachius*

I extol virginity to the skies, not because I myself possess it, but because, not possessing it, I admire it all the more.

—Jerome, *Letter to Pammachius*

The apostle says, "Now as to virgins, I have no precept of the Lord, but I give my advice." When, therefore, he simply gives advice about maintaining virginity, and lays down no precept, he acknowledges that it is above the commandment. Those, therefore, who preserve virginity, do more than the commandment requires. But it will then only profit you to have done more than was commanded, if you also do that which *is* commanded.

—Sulpitius Severus, *Letter to Claudia*

If I have called virginity gold, I have spoken of marriage as silver.

—Jerome, *Letter to Pammachius*

Caution

Remember Adam and Eve fell when they were virgins, and that the perfect purity of their bodies did not profit them when they sinned.

—Sulpitius Severus, *Letter to Claudia*

I will say it boldly, though God can do all things He cannot raise up a virgin when once she has fallen.

—Jerome, *Letter to Eustochium*

O virgin, do not flatter yourself on the ground of your purity alone, and do not trust in the perfection of one member; but according to the apostle, maintain the sanctity of your body throughout.

—Sulpitius Severus, *Letter to Claudia*

Virginity may be lost even by a thought.

—Jerome, *Letter to Eustochium*

Virtue

Virtue is nothing but well-directed love.

—Augustine

Virtue is not the knowing of good and evil. Rather, virtue is the doing of good and not-doing of evil.

—Lactantius, *The Divine Institutions*

Nothing is more harmless than the man who is perfect in virtue.

—Augustine, *Our Lord's Sermon on the Mount*

There are . . . three things which enable men to control their faults; viz., either the fear of hell or of laws even now imposed; or the hope and desire of the Kingdom of heaven; or a liking for goodness itself and the love of virtue.

—John Cassian, *The First Conference of Abbot Chaeremon*

N.B.

Let us not imitate the faults of one whose virtues we cannot equal.

—Jerome, *Letter to Pammachius and Oceanus*

War

Let us make war with our enemies with prayers and supplications.

—John Chrysostom, *Homilies on Thessalonians*

Murder is a crime if one person commits it; but it is acclaimed as virtuous and brave if many commit it!

—Cyprian

But beyond doubt it is greater felicity to have a good neighbour at peace, than to conquer a bad one by making war.

—Augustine, *The City of God*

Will of God

Nothing, therefore, happens unless the Omnipotent wills it to happen: He either permits it to happen, or He brings it about Himself.

—Augustine

The will of God is the measure of things.

—Ambrose of Milan

It is enough indeed to lay it down, that nothing happens without the will of God.

—Tertullian, *De Fuga in Persecutione*

God "wills all men to be saved"; but that is if they come to Him. For He does not will that they be saved who do not want to be saved. He wills that they be saved if they themselves also will it.

—Ambrose of Milan, *Commentaries on Thirteen Pauline Epistles*

God is capable of willing, but not of not willing.

—Hippolytus, *Discourse on the Divine Nature*

For whether it goes well with you or whether it goes ill, yet His will is going to be done *in* you. But would that it be done also *by* you!

—Augustine, *The Lord's Prayer Explained*

Wisdom

Wisdom is intelligence, but all intelligence is not wisdom.

—Clement of Alexandria, *The Stromata*

Wishing to describe the different kinds of wisdom, he (the apostle) points out that there is a wisdom of this world, and a wisdom of the princes of this world, and another wisdom of God.

—Origen, *De Principiis*

Worldly wisdom differs (from divine) just to the measure that truth differs from plausibility.

—Athenagoras, *A Plea Regarding Christians*

Almost all bodily excellencies alter with age, and while wisdom alone increases all things else decay.

—Jerome, *Letter to Nepotian*

We must not detract from the virtues of our opponents . . . but neither must we praise the defects of our friends.

—Jerome, *Letter to Pammachius and Oceanus*

The wise man must be useful to many; so that he who is useful only to himself cannot be wise.

—Hippolytus, *Commentary on Proverbs*

N.B.

He is not wise enough to think little of himself.

—Jerome, *Letter to Oceanus*

Witness

He can never be at a loss for words who has believed on the Word.

—Jerome, *Letter to Innocent*

Blind and lame bear witness, and dead men raised to life, and devils saying, "We know Thee, Who Thou art, the Holy One of God." Winds bear witness, silenced at His bidding: five loaves multiplied into five thousand bear Him witness. The holy wood of the Cross bears witness. . . . The palm-tree on the ravine bears witness, having supplied the palm-branches to the children who then hailed Him. Gethsemane bears witness. . . . Golgotha, the holy hill standing above us here, bears witness . . . the Holy Sepulchre bears witness, and the stone which lies there to this day. The sun now shining is His witness, which then at the time of His saving Passion was eclipsed: the darkness is His witness, which was then from the sixth hour to the ninth: the light bears witness, which shone forth from the ninth hour until evening. The Mount of Olives bears witness . . . the rain-bearing clouds are His witnesses . . . yea, and the gates of heaven bear witness.

. . . His former enemies bear witness . . . the twelve apostles are His witnesses . . . the shadow of Peter bears witness . . . the handkerchiefs and aprons bear witness . . . Persians and Goths, and all the Gentile converts bear witness, by dying for His sake, whom they never saw with eyes of flesh.

—Cyril of Jerusalem, *Lecture X*

Women

True nobility

Women who wear gold ornaments are evidently afraid that without their ornaments or stripped of their jewelry they might be taken for slaves. True nobility, however, is found in the beauty and substance of the soul.

—Clement of Alexandria, *The Instructor*

Let them be well clothed—without by raiment, within by modesty.

—Clement of Alexandria, *The Instructor*

Speak to my sisters, that they love in the Lord, and that their husbands be sufficient for them in the flesh and spirit.

—Ignatius, *Epistle to Polycarp*

It is your duty to please your husbands, and your husbands alone. The less you trouble to please other men, the more you will please them.

—Tertullian, *On Female Dress*

For the very shadow of a husband is a wife's safeguard.

—Jerome, *Letter to Salvina*

Always bear in mind that it was a woman who expelled the tiller of paradise from his heritage.

—Jerome, *Letter to Nepotian*

The weaker sex?

And if thou sayest that it attacked her as being the weaker of the two, (I reply that) on the contrary, she was the stronger, since she appears to have been the helper of the man in the transgression of the commandment. For she did by herself alone resist the serpent, and it was after holding out for a while and making opposition that she ate of the tree, being circumvented by craft; whereas Adam, making no fight whatever, nor refusal, partook of the fruit handed to him by the woman, which is an indication of the utmost imbecility and effeminacy of mind. And the woman indeed, having been vanquished in the contest by a demon, is deserving of pardon; but Adam shall deserve none, for he was worsted by a woman.

—Irenaeus, *Fragments from Lost Writings*

N.B.

A man ought by all means to fly from women and bishops.

—John Cassian, *The Institutes*

Word

What was in the beginning? "The Word," he says. . . . Why the Word? So that we might know that He proceeded from the mind. Why the Word? Because he was begotten without passion. Why the Word? Because He is Image of the Father who begets Him. . . .

—Basil the Great, *Sermon on "In the beginning was the Word"*

...for there was no word before the Word.

—Gregory of Nazianzus, *On the Theophany*

Power of a word

The mystics say that it was by his word alone that Moses slew the Egyptian; as certainly afterwards it is related in the Acts that (Peter) slew with his word those who kept back part of the price of the land, and lied.

—Clement of Alexandria, *Fragments*

Works

(See also: Goodness)

Importance of works

Do not presume to teach anyone in words what you have not already performed in deed. For our Lord . . . "began to do and to teach."

—John Cassian, *The First Conference of Abbot Nesteros*

Wells, when pumped out, yield purer water; and that of which no one partakes, turns to putrefaction. Use keeps steel brighter, but disuse produces rust. . . .

—Clement of Alexandria, *The Stromata*

Perish the thought that there is any true virtue in anyone who is not just.

—Augustine, *Against Julian*

We contend here, we are crowned elsewhere.

—Jerome, *Letter to Eustochium*

Faith and works

Those very works, which are said to have been done prior to faith, although they appear to men to be praiseworthy, are really in vain. It seems to me that they are like the great power of the swiftest runner, whose race, however, is on the wrong track.

—Augustine, *Psalms*

Works are the consequences rather than the precedents of grace. Thus, no man is to suppose that he has received grace because he has done good works but rather that he would not have been able to do those good works if he had not, through faith, received grace.

—Augustine, *Various Questions to Simplician*

Nobody must boast of the good works he did before he had faith; nobody must be sluggish in doing good works now that faith is his.

—Augustine, *Psalms 31*

N.B.

When God crowns our merits, He is crowning nothing else but His own gifts to us.

—Augustine, *Grace and Free Choice*

Worldliness

The world is God's, but the worldly is the devil's.

—Tertullian

Somehow or other those please the world most who please Christ least.

—Jerome, *Letter to Paulinus*

Worship

God only . . .

I will . . . honour the king. . . . But God . . . I worship.

—Theophilus of Antioch, *To Autolycus*

Misdirected worship

We neither worship crosses nor wish for them.

—Minucius Felix, *Octavius*

The sun and moon were made for us; how, then, can I adore my own servants?

—Tatian, *Address to the Greeks*

N.B.

By what image am I to represent God, since, rightly considered, man himself is the image of God? What temple am I to erect to Him, since the whole of this world which has been fashioned by Him, is unable to contain Him?

—Minucius Felix, *Octavius*

Youth

Age—relative

Daniel the wise, at twelve years of age, became possessed of the Divine Spirit, and convicted the elders, who in vain carried their grey hairs, of being false accusers. . . . Samuel alas when he was but a child reproved Eli, who was ninety years old, for giving honour to his sons rather than to God. In like manner Jeremiah also received this message from God, "Say not I am a child." Solomon too, and Josiah . . . the former being made king at twelve years of age, gave that terrible and difficult judgment in the case of the two women concerning their children. The latter, coming to the throne when eight years old cast down the altars and temples (of the idols), and burned down the groves, for they were dedicated to demons, and not to God. . . . Wherefore youth is not to be despised when it is devoted to God. But he is to be despised who is of a wicked mind, although he be old, and full of wicked days. Timothy the Christ-bearer was young, but look what his teacher writes to him: "Let no man despise thy youth. . . ."

—Ignatius, *Epistle to the Magnesians*

As a boy, Daniel judges old men and in the flower of youth condemns the incontinence of age.

—Jerome, *Letter to Paulinus*

Blaesilla . . . fulfilled in a short time of life a long time of virtue.

—Jerome, *Letter to Furia*

Temptations

Wine is the first weapon used by demons against the young.

—Jerome, *Letter to Eustochium*

Neither the fiery Etna nor the country of Vulcan, nor Vesuvius, nor Olympus, burns with such violent heat as the youthful marrow of those who are flushed with wine and filled with food.

—Jerome, *Letter to Furia*

N.B.

In the lives of Christians we look not to the beginnings but to the endings. Paul began badly but ended well. The start of Judas wins praise; his end is condemned. . . .

—Jerome, *Letter to Furia*

Biographies

ALEXANDER, of Alexandria (circa 328 A.D.). Bishop of Alexandria, and a key figure at the Council of Nicea in 325 A.D. It was during his time that the Arian controversy arose.

AMBROSE, (340–397 A.D.). Bishop of Milan. Exemplary in both his private and public life. His powerful preaching so influenced Augustine that he became a Christian. He wrote many scriptual and dogmatic works, and has been called the "Father of Latin Hymnody."

AMPHILOCHIUS, of Iconium (313–394 A.D.). Close friend of the Great Cappadocians. Bishop of Iconium. A capable administrator and a prominent participant in the theological controversies of his time. He wrote extensively, but most of his work has been lost.

APHRAATES, the Persian sage (280–345 A.D.). The oldest of the "fathers" of the Syrian church. An ascetic; probably a bishop.

ARISTIDES, of Athens (circa 140 A.D.). We have only scant information on him, but he was considered to be a Christian philosopher. According to Eusebius, he was a "man of faith and devoted to our religion."

ARNOBIUS, of Sicca (327 A.D.). For many years a vigorous opponent of Christianity. After his conversion, his bishop was skeptical and demanded proof of sincerity. To offer such proof Arnobius wrote seven books against the pagans.

ATHANASIUS, (298–373 A.D.). Born in Alexandria. Played a pivotal role at the Council of Nicea. Lifelong defender of orthodoxy against the Arians. Five times exiled. Bishop of Alexandria.

ATHENAGORAS, of Athens (circa 180 A.D.). Very little is known of him, except that he was a Christian philosopher and lived in Athens. A contemporary of Justin Martyr and Tatian.

AUGUSTINE, Aurelius (354–430 A.D.). The great Western Father. Bishop of Hippo. "The richest mind in Christendom." The most prolific author in the Western Church. His most famous works: *Confessions, The City of God, De Trinitate.*

BARDESANES, (154–223 A.D.). Born of noble parents in Edessa. Later retired to Armenia. He composed many hymns.

BARNABAS, (either 70–79 or 117–132 A.D.). Author of the *Letter of Barnabas*, which is more of a theological tract than a letter. From earliest times he was identified as Barnabas of the New Testament and companion of Paul, but such authorship is not tenable. The book is un-Pauline in character. According to the *Codex Sinaiticus* it was included in the works of the New Testament.

BASIL, the Great (330–379 A.D.). One of ten children, three of whom became bishops. One of the "Great Cappadocians." Lifelong friend of Gregory of Nazianzus: it was said of them, they were "one soul with two bodies." Bishop of Caesarea. A gifted writer and a man firm in resolve. Together with John Chrysostom he is accounted one of the two pillars of the Oriental Church.

BOETHIUS, (480–524 A.D.). Made consul by the king of Rome, but later was imprisoned at Pavia, and put to death—partly for his Christian faith. While in prison he wrote the *Consolation of Philosophy*, the best known of his works.

CAESAR, of Arles (470–542 A.D.). An influential Gallic bishop, and probably the greatest moral preacher in the Western Church of his day. A strong anti-Pelagist, he was also renowned for his works of charity, living himself in complete poverty.

CASSIAN, John (360–435 A.D.). Probably a native of Gaul but spent many years in Egypt studying asceticism and monasticism. Ordained to the diaconate by Chrysostom; and later ordained a priest. Founded two monasteries in Marseilles. A "Semi-Pelagian" but vehemently rejected Pelagianism.

CHRYSOSTOM, John (345–407 A.D.). One of the greatest of the Fathers of the church. Bishop of Constantinople. Outspoken reformer, great orator and eloquent preacher. He was given the name of "Chrysostom"—the gold mouth. Died in exile.

CLEMENT, of Alexandria (150–220 A.D.). Born in Athens but forever associated with the church in Alexandria. One of the first of the great leaders in Africa. He was also the first to explore in his writings the relations between faith and reason.

CLEMENT, of Rome (30–100 A.D.). Probably a Gentile and a Roman. He seems to have been at Philippi with Paul. A co-presbyter with Linus and Cletus, he became their successor in government of the Roman Church.

COMMODIANUS, (circa 240 A.D.). Very little is known of him except that he was a North African bishop. From his writings it can be deduced that his beliefs reflected those of a primitive age; his language a "wretched patois"; his personal piety and earnestness beyond dispute.

CYPRIAN, Thascius Caecilius (200–258 A.D.). Native of North Africa. Great lawyer and orator.

CYRIL, of Jerusalem (315–386 A.D.). Consecrated bishop of Jerusalem by Acacius the Arian metropolitan of Caesarea. Cyril, however, was a defender of Nicene doctrine. His career was a stormy one—not orthodox enough for the orthodox, not Arian enough for the Arians. Expelled three times from his see.

DAMASCENE, John (645–749 A.D.). Also known as John Chrysorrhoas, the Golden Speaker. Born in Damascus, and died in the monastery of Mar Saba, near Jerusalem. Always orthodox in his theology, and Chalcedonian in his Christology. A fluent preacher and a prolific author. It is claimed that he had 150 titles listed to his name.

DAMASUS, pope from 366–384 A.D. It was he who commissioned Jerome's translation of the Scriptures, and who changed the liturgical language of the Roman Church from Greek to Latin.

DIDYMUS, the Blind (313–398 A.D.). Born in Alexandria; blind from the age of four; lived to become one of the most learned men and one of the most prolific writers of his age. Head of the catechetical school of Alexandria, appointed by Athanasius. One of his most famous pupils was Jerome.

DIONYSIUS, the Great (248–265 A.D.). One of Origen's most remarkable pupils, and succeeded him as bishop of Alexandria.

EPHRAIM, the Syrian (306–373 A.D.). Sometime called the "lyre of the Holy Spirit." A great classic author of the Syrian Church. Most of his work was in poetic form.

EPIPHANIUS, of Salamis (315–403 A.D.). Born near Gaza in Palestine. Bishop of Salamis on the island of Cyprus. Jerome called him a Pentaglot, because of his knowledge of Hebrew, Syriac, Greek, Coptic, and Latin. He hated Origen; was sadly lacking in tact and judgment; but demonstrated great zeal for Nicene orthodoxy.

EUSEBIUS, (260–339 A.D.). The bishop of Caesarea, friend of the emperor Constantine. "Father of Church History." Authored many exegetical and doctrinal works, and in particular, his monumental *Church History*.

EVAGRIUS, of Pontus (345–399 A.D.). Ordained a lector by Basil the Great, but spent many years in a self-imposed exile in the deserts of Egypt. Much of his work has been lost, probably because he was condemned as an Origenist at the Fifth Ecumenical Council, 533 A.D.

FAUSTINUS (flourished circa 380 A.D.). A priest in Rome and a Luciferian. This meant that he was adamant, to the point of being a schismatic, for the Nicene doctrine. An indefatigable opponent of Arianism.

FELIX, Marcus Minucius (Third century). Distinguished lawyer of African origin. A convert to Christianity from Stoicism.

FIRMIANUS, Lactantius (260–340 A.D.). Survived the Diocletian persecution and became tutor of Constantine's son. A native of Numidia, Africa.

FULGENCE, of Ruspe (467–527 A.D.) A one time tax-collector in his native town in North Africa. Became a monk and finally bishop of Ruspe. Exiled for many years to Sardinia in the Arian-Vandal persecution. Probably one of the greatest theologians of his age, and is one in his doctrine with Augustine. He would not subscribe to the immaculate conception of the Virgin Mary.

GREGORY, of Elvira (392 A.D.). Bishop of Elvira. Strong against Arianism. Highly praised by Jerome.

GREGORY, the Great (540–604 A.D.). Born to a rich and noble family, he withdrew from the world, sold his goods and built seven monasteries with the proceeds. He was brought out of the monastery and unanimously chosen pope. He fought heresy, enforced ecclesiastical discipline, and through a missionary called Augustine evangelized Great Britain. He was one of only two popes given the title "the great." He styled himself *servus servorum Dei*.

GREGORY, the Miracle-worker (213–275 A.D.). Student of Origen, he became bishop of Neocaesarea. Reputed to be the founder of the church in Cappadocia.

GREGORY, of Nazianzus (330–394 A.D.). The second of the three great Cappadocian Fathers. Very close friend of Basil the Great. Bishop of Nazianzus. A gentle and peaceful man; his writings reveal great theological insight and were highly esteemed.

GREGORY, of Nyssa (335–394 A.D.). Younger brother of Basil the Great, and the third of the Three Cappadocians. A mystic, a theologian, and exceptionally gifted as a writer. Bishop of Nyssa.

GREGORY, Thaumaturgus (213–275 A.D.). Born of wealthy parents; he took the name "Gregory" on his conversion and baptism to Christianity. First bishop of his native city, Neocaesarea. Some claim that he was the founder of the church in Cappadocia. Many refer to him as a great miracle-worker, hence "Thaumaturgus."

HERMAS, (140 A.D.). Author of "The Shepherd," a book that was in general circulation both in the Eastern and Western churches. Some believe him to be the Hermas greeted by Paul in Romans 16:14. Others, that he was Hermas the brother of Pope Pius I.

HILARY, (died 367 A.D.). Bishop of Poitiers. Credited with being the most learned man in Gaul. He stoutly defended orthodox Christology against the onslaughts of Arianism. Author of the book, *De Trinitate*.

HIPPOLYTUS, (170–236 A.D.). Greek by birth; disciple of Irenaeus; a Roman bishop. He withstood the contemporary bishops of Rome for their error of doctrine, misconduct and the quality of their lifestyle. His most important work: "The Refutation of All Heresies." Saint, scholar, martyr.

IGNATIUS, (died circa 117 A.D.). Bishop of Antioch. Little is known of him except what we can glean from his letters and from Eusebius. An exceptionally courageous martyr; a strong advocate of episcopacy; a consistent opponent of heresy and schism.

IRENAEUS, of Lyons (115–202 A.D.). Bishop of Lyons in Southern Gaul. Born in Smyrna and taught by Polycarp. A man of much wisdom; a noted polemicist; a champion of orthodoxy.

ISIDORE, of Seville (560–636 A.D.). Bishop of Seville. The last of the Fathers of the West. A compiler, possibly "the greatest compiler there has ever been." Highly esteemed as a person, but much of his work came to be regarded as superficial.

JEROME, (347–420 A.D.). A careful historian and great scholar. Translator of the Bible into Latin—the Vulgate. His work was initially criticized but later was widely acclaimed. A scholar and saint but also a man of some arrogance and biting sarcasm. A zealous promoter of the monastic life.

JUSTIN, Martyr (100–165 A.D.). One of the earliest and best known of the Apologists. Native of Syria. Beheaded, with six other Christians in Rome.

LEPORIUS. Under Augustine's influence he gave up all his property and the temporal care of a monastery, and built a house of refuge for strangers in Hippo. He also, at his own expense, built a church in memory of the "eight martyrs."

LUCIAN, (125-190 A.D.). Born in Samosata in Northern Syria. Settled in Athens and wrote numerous works.

MACARIUS, the Magnesian (circa 400 A.D.). It is said that at the Synod of the Oak (403) he was the accuser of Heraclides, bishop of Ephesus. He was probably the author of *Only-Begotten Christ Himself to the Pagans.*

MARIUS VICTORINUS, born in 300 A.D. in Africa. Became an orator in Rome; later converted to Christianity. Jerome claimed that his writings were very obscure and could only be understood by the learned.

MELITO, of Sardis (latter half of second century). Bishop of Sardis. Addressed an *Apology* for Christians to Marcus Aurelius.

METHODIUS, of Olympus (died circa 311 A.D.). Bishop of Olympus and Patara, and later of Tyre. Martyred in the Diocletian persecution.

NESTORIUS, (381–453 A.D.). Born of Persian parents; received his theological training in the School of Antioch. A most eloquent preacher, elevated by the Emperor to the see of Constantinople. He argued strongly against calling Mary *Theotokos* (mother of God). He referred to her as *Christotokos* (mother of Christ). At the Third Ecumenical Council in Ephesus, Nestorius was condemned as a heretic, and driven into exile.

NOVATIAN, (210–280 A.D.). A presbyter in Rome. Hard-liner on the question of leniency to the lapsed. On this matter he opposed Pope Cornelius and became known as an anti-pope, and his sect spread with some success in Spain and Syria. He refused any reconciliation to those who had lapsed from the faith.

OPTATUS, of Milevis (320–385 A.D.). Bishop of Milevis in Numidian Africa. Little is known about him, except that he wrote on the Catholic side against the Donatists. He was regarded as a sincere man of simple faith.

ORIGEN, of Adamantius (185–255 A.D.). At eighteen he was chosen head of the Catechetical School in Alexandria. Lived an exceedingly rigorous and ascetic life—sleeping on bare boards, fasted frequently. . . . He was imprisoned and tortured during the Decian persecution. He authored numerous books; no fewer than 2,000 books, according to Jerome. Because of some of his teachings, the Roman Catholic Church labelled him a heretic in 399 A.D.

PACIAN, of Barcelona (inter 379–393 A.D.). Bishop of Barcelona. According to Jerome, he was a man whose life was more illustrious than his words. Not particularly original as a writer, but had a delightful style. He defended the Catholic Church against Novatianism.

PAPIAS, (70–155 A.D.). Bishop of Hierapolis in Phrygia. He knew and was associated with the Apostle John, and others "who had seen the Lord." He worked in close association with Polycarp; wrote five books—all lost. A martyr.

PECTORIUS,(350–400 A.D.). Known only by his epitaph. The symbol of the fish is prominent throughout the whole epitaph.

PETER, of Alexandria (260–311 A.D.). Bishop of Alexandria, noted for both his learning and knowledge of the Scriptures, and for the sanctity of his life. He took a decided stand against heresy; became a martyr in the persecution unleashed by Maximin.

PLINY THE YOUNGER, (62–113 A.D.). Nephew of the distinguished naturalist and writer, the elder Pliny. The emperor Trajan made him governor of Bithynia.

POLYCARP, (69–155 A.D.). A disciple of the Apostle John; he had met and talked with people who had actually known Jesus. He was made bishop of Smyrna while quite young. A heroic martyr.

PROSPER, of Acquitaine (died 463 A.D.). A layman of Southern Gaul. He obtained from the pope a letter confirming the orthodoxy of Augustine, and begged the Gallican bishops to end their campaign against him.

SALVIAN, fifth century priest at Marseilles. His most famous work was his book, *The Governance of God.*

SERAPION, (circa 350 A.D.). Bishop of Thmuis in Egypt. The Sacramentary attributed to him consists of some thirty prayers.

SEVERUS, a bishop of Antioch in the sixth century.

SIDONIUS, Apollinaris (430–487 A.D.). Bishop of Clermont. Poet and letter-writer.

SIXTUS II. One of the early popes in Rome.

SYNESIUS, (373–414 A.D.). A native of Cyrene. Bishop of Ptolemais. Friend of Hypatia, the woman philosopher of Alexandria.

TATIAN, the Syrian (circa 170 A.D.). Very little is known of his life, even less of his death. Born into paganism, he sought the true philosophy and found it in the Christian faith. He is best remembered for his *Harmony of the Gospels* (Diatessaron) and his *Address to the Greeks.*

TERTULLIAN, (160–230 A.D.). Native of Carthage. He was attracted by the asceticism of Montanism, but finally broke with them and with the Church and founded his own sect. A superb writer—apologetical, dogmatic and controversial.

THEODORE, of Mopsuestia (circa 428 A.D.). Fellow student of Chrysostom, and was greatly influenced by him. Bishop of Mopsuestia in Cilicia. Suspected of being tainted with Nestorianism, he was condemned at the Fifth Ecumenical Council of Constantinople, 533 A.D. Modern research seriously doubts if he was ever a "Nestorian," and his works that have survived reveal no such evidence.

THEONAS, of Alexandria (circa 300 A.D.). Bishop of Alexandria for nineteen years. His only work that is extant is his letter to Lucianus, the chief chamberlain to the emperor.

THEOPHILUS, of Antioch (185–211 A.D.). Born near the Euphrates; converted as an adult through studying the Scriptures. Became the seventh bishop of Antioch. Very little is known of him except what one gleans from his book, *To Autolycus.*

VINCENT, of Lerins (died 450 A.D.). Of Gallic nationality. First a soldier, then a monk. Retired to the monastery of Lerins where he wrote the Commonitory. References made to him by Cardinal Newman, Pope Pius X, and the Vatican Council.

ZACHARY, of Mitylene (533 A.D.). Also known as Zachary Scholastikos and Zachary the Rhetor. Born near Gaza, and ended as Metropolitan Bishop of Mitylene. He subscribed to the condemnation of Severus and other Monophysites.

The OMEGA Conspiracy

I. D. E. Thomas

The burgeoning of demonic activity in our time is proof of our proximity to the "last days" and to the mightiest power encounter of all history. The "sons of God" are on a collision course with the saints of God, and we may well be witnessing the opening scenario.

THE EVIDENCE MOUNTS

More and we are finding that mythology in general though greatly contorted very often has some historic base. And the interesting thing is that one myth which occurs over and over again in many parts of the world is that somewhere a long time ago supernatural beings had sexual [relations] with natural women and produced a special breed of people.

—Francis A. Schaeffer

WARNINGS FROM THE PAST

Do we ever learn from history? What were the conditions on the Earth that resulted in its destruction except for Noah and his family? What are the conditions on the Earth today? Will history repeat itself in our time? I. D. E. Thomas reveals startling similarities between the past and today; between ancient peoples and modern peoples. *THE OMEGA CONSPIRACY* could well be the final battle.

ISBN 0-9624517-4-6 254 pages

PURITAN DAILY DEVOTIONAL CHRONICLES

I. D. E. Thomas

Puritanism, as a Christian attitude and conviction regarding faith, service, and doctrinal purity, can be dated to the 1550s. The Puritans were known as scholars and theologians who thought that the Protestant Reformation, and subsequently, the Church of England, had not gone far enough in purging out the leaven of papacy and Roman Catholicism.

These churchmen sought to further reform the church to teach and preach only the Gospel of Jesus Christ and biblical truths as set forth in the New Testament and further declared in the Pauline revelation.

Though some Puritans were involved in the work of the King James Bible, the King disliked the Puritans and threatened to exterminate them; therefore, they were among those who first came to the new land seeking religious freedom. Puritans like John Adams, John Harvard, and Johnathan Edwards were instrumental in forming the educational, governmental, and spiritual foundations of the United States.

This book of devotions by some of the most noted Puritans in history are daily reminders that we must return to our foundational roots if America is to prosper and endure.

ISBN 1-879366-99-1 **381 pages**